TAKE CONTROL
OF YOUR DIVORCE

TAKE CONTROL OF YOUR DIVORCE

STRATEGIES TO STOP FIGHTING & START CO-PARENTING

JUDITH MARGERUM, PH.D.
JEROME A. PRICE, M.A.
JAMES WINDELL, M.A.

Impact **Publishers**®
ATASCADERO, CALIFORNIA

ATTENTION ORGANIZATIONS AND CORPORATIONS:
This book is available at quantity discounts on bulk purchases for educational, business, or sales promotional use. For further information, please contact Impact Publishers, P.O. Box 6016, Atascadero, California 93423-6016. Phone: 805-466-5917, e-mail: info@impactpublishers.com

Library of Congress Cataloging-in-Publication Data

Margerum, Judith.
    Take control of your divorce : strategies to stop fighting & start co-parenting / Judith Margerum, Jerome A. Price, James Windell.
        p. cm.
    Includes bibliographical references and index.
    ISBN 978-1-886230-97-2 (alk. paper)
  1. Divorced parents. 2. Parenting. 3. Children of divorced parents. I. Price, Jerome A. II. Windell, James. III. Title.
    HQ759.915.M356 2010
    306.89—dc22

                                                                        2010039388

Publisher's Note: This publication is designed to provide accurate and authoritative information in regard to the subject matter covered. It is sold with the understanding that the publisher is not engaged in rendering psychological, medical, legal, or other professional services. If expert assistance or counseling is needed, the services of a competent professional should be sought.

Impact strives to make our books readable, grammatically correct, and free of gender bias. Thus, we alternate feminine and masculine pronouns rather than use the cumbersome "he or she" combination, or the popular — if incorrect — "they."

Impact Publishers and colophon are registered trademarks of Impact Publishers, Inc.

Cover design by Gayle Downs, Gayle Force Design, Atascadero, California
Composition by UB Communications, Parsippany, New Jersey
Printed in the United States of America on acid-free, recycled paper
Published by **Impact 🕊 Publishers®**
POST OFFICE BOX 6016
ATASCADERO, CALIFORNIA 93423-6016
www.impactpublishers.com

Dedications

To all the families that I have worked with who allowed me to help them navigate such a major life event. And to my own co-parent and children who have shown me how important it is to put the children first.

— J. M.

For Josh, Nathaniel and Seth — my boys, who I'd do anything for.

— J. P.

To Jane, the love of my life.

— J. W.

CONTENTS

Acknowledgments

I t would have been impossible to put together the extensive body of knowledge we base this book on without the support, trust, and referral of families by the judges, referees, and family counselors of the Family Division of the Sixth Judicial Circuit Court in Oakland County, Michigan. Their collective support of our non-adversarial approaches to traditional divorce problems is what makes new ideas and creative solutions possible.

The Family Division judges of the Sixth Circuit Court have consistently supported our work and our efforts to help people who come before them with seemingly irreconcilable differences. We appreciate the work of all of our judges: Judge James Alexander, Judge Mary Ellen Brennan, Judge Lisa Gorcyca, Judge Linda Hallmark, Judge Cheryl Matthews, Judge Eugene Moore, Judge Elizabeth Pezzetti, and Judge Joan Young.

Also in the Sixth Circuit Court, we owe a deep debt of gratitude to Court Services Manager Pamela Davis, who has always welcomed new ideas and programs with enthusiasm and sage advice. We have been blessed to have her as both an administrator and partner in listening to our suggestions and making them even better with her insightful comments and ideas. Additionally, the Friend of the Court, Suzanne Hollyer, along with the referees and the family counselors in the Friend of the Court division, have been very helpful and responsive to our needs and are always available to consult on the difficult cases. We especially want to acknowledge the wonderful working relationships we've enjoyed over the years with Referee Libby Blanchard, Referee Suzanne Bolton, and Referee Mark Sherbow, as well as with the following family counselors: Mary Kaye Neumann, Brian Gallant, Sandra Binder, Sue McCoy, Katherine Stahl, Terry Oppenheim, Katie

Dopke, Jane McCarron, Vicki Rupert, Jody LaPointe, Lori Klein-Shapiro, Joe Rzepecki, Beverly Green, Kathleen Doan, Tracey Stieb, and Jany Lee-Warren.

In the ADEPT program in the Circuit Court, Mary Seyuin has been a skilled colleague and friend for James for many years. He appreciates her cheerfulness and her patient approach to the clients who require extra clinical tools, and he acknowledges how much he has learned from working with her in the often intense and difficult clinical relationship they share in daily work with high-conflict divorce couples.

In addition, we are most thankful to all of the divorcing and divorced co-parents who have had the courage to step out of the traditional path and find compassionate and supportive ways of dealing with each other. They make it possible for their children to be truly happy and successful. Their resilience and ultimate ability to change makes up for the initial anger they bring to our sessions. There is no question that there is always something more to learn from clinical work with this constantly challenging population of parents. The problems that they present to us, while at times frustrating, are also the reason why we find our work life filled with new territories to explore and challenges to be met. They keep us on our toes and force us to constantly try to grasp new concepts, learn new approaches, and figure out new solutions to difficult problems.

Finally, we want to extend a heart-felt thanks to Melissa Froehner at Impact Publishers, Inc., for her support when we presented the concept of this book to her initially, and her helpful suggestions throughout the project. It has been a real pleasure to work with a publishing company that cares about its authors and goes out of its way to make life easier.

Introduction

If you and your co-parent have been separated or divorced for more than a year or two and you aren't working together in a spirit of cooperation for the good of your children, then you likely understand that something is wrong.

During our many years as psychotherapists working with people in high-conflict relationships following separation or divorce, we've honed and refined many effective techniques and strategies to help people get through these trying periods. Being human, there's a limited number of individuals and couples the three of us can work with on an individual basis, but, as we are constantly reminded, there are many couples who endure bitter and hostile relationships after divorce. We've written this book in hopes of sharing our techniques with those who need them.

Therapists and mediators use these strategies in their practices, but there's no reason you can't use them as well. That's what this book is about. It's about you putting these counseling and therapy strategies to work for you. You can learn the methods, understand the theory behind them, and apply them to your own situation with your co-parent.

Take Control of Your Divorce is divided into five sections. Section I introduces you to high-conflict divorces and high-conflict relationships. If you continue to fight, you're in a dangerous rut — dangerous because of the likely effects on your children. Children in the center of postdivorce conflict are at considerable risk for suffering physically, emotionally, and behaviorally. Far too often, we see families in which a divorce took place many years before they came to us, but the conflicts have continued and the teenaged children are involved in mental health services or the juvenile court or they are estranged from one or both parents. We don't want this to happen to your children. This book tells you the steps to take to protect your children from these misfortunes.

Sections II and III present the strategies to resolve, overlook, or put aside the conflicts with your co-parent so you can go about the more important task of being good parents. You'll find techniques to change yourself and techniques to change your co-parent. Among the strategies you'll find in these two sections are those that help you let go of your anger, bring yourself to apologize to your co-parent, forgive your co-parent, use your children in a positive way to help resolve problems with your co-parent, and create a healing ritual.

Many couples in high-conflict relationships have an angry and unproductive communication cycle based on the ineffective emotions of anger, resentment, hostility, and rage. In chapter 15 in section III, we show you how you can end that cycle. Change the way you communicate with your co-parent, and you change yourself — you just may change your co-parent as well.

We discuss how to deal with a co-parent with special needs in chapter 16 in section IV. Whether your ex's problem is related to mental illness, substance abuse, or domestic violence, life can be very frustrating for you as you attempt to share parenting responsibilities. In this chapter you will learn how to make sure that you properly assess your ex's special needs and then develop a plan of action.

We wrap up this book in the final section by reviewing how to be successful co-parents despite your differences. We know from our clinical experience over many years with many different couples locked in hostile relationships that you can go from a relationship featuring anger and hostility to one that is less volatile, more cooperative, and healthier for your children. Our most basic intent for this book is to help you save your children — and yourself — from the ravages of anger, hostility, and conflict.

Your co-parent doesn't have to also read this book. However, if he or she does (don't hesitate to buy a second copy to send as a gift — maybe anonymously!), there is an even better chance that the two of you can work together to make your co-parenting successful.

If You're Still Fighting After the Divorce Is Over, You Are Still Emotionally Married

CHAPTER 1

If You're Still Fighting, Then You're Stuck in a Rut!

In the ideal divorce — if there is such an animal — you give up your anger and hostility toward your former spouse relatively quickly, accept that you must be cooperative partners in raising your children, and move on with your life. Divorce, however, isn't always ideal.

> When Amanda got a divorce from Louis, she thought it would be the end of their stormy relationship.
>
> "Louis was always such a jerk about trying to control me," Amanda told a friend. "Now that we're divorced, he'll never be able to tell me what to do again."
>
> But Amanda and Louis had two children, Maria and Leo. Instead of ending the relationship, Amanda soon discovered that she and Louis were still very much involved with each other, as they had to talk to each other frequently regarding the children.
>
> "He still tries to run my life!" Amanda complains. "He uses the children to exert power over me. Louis says it's what's good for the kids, but I know he just has to make sure *I* do what *he* wants."

And that's the grand illusion of divorce. Like Amanda, many people think the relationship will be over once the judge signs the divorce decree. Only later do they find that they are as emotionally tied to one another as ever because of their mutual responsibilities for raising their children. One relationship ends, but a new one begins, and although it's no longer a marriage, this relationship is just as real and as challenging as the one you had before the divorce.

To think you are done with that other person is a fantasy. As long as you have children, there will be a relationship. And as long as you have children, you will be co-parents with all the potential for conflict that existed before the divorce. Some people think they can end it by not talking to the ex-spouse. The fact is that this makes the drama more intense. And, with the drama comes a more intense attachment. You don't give the silent treatment to someone you're really done with.

So, if you are nowhere near the ideal in your divorce, if you are still fighting with your ex-spouse, and if your conflicts make you just as angry as before the divorce, you may still be emotionally married.

Emotional Marriage

Being *emotionally married* means you still have strong feelings — both positive and negative — toward your ex. This is the case with Marco and Anita:

> Marco and Anita have been divorced for four years, and Marco still feels their parenting time is not divided fairly, as he does not have the kids fifty percent of the time. He believes that Anita monopolizes their three children's free time, schedules things without consulting him, and tries to control both the children and him. The parenting coordinator hoped that by getting Anita to give in on several significant parenting time issues, they might be able to start anew. The coordinator was able to convince Anita of the potential good that might come if Marco could see that she was beginning to compromise by including him more as a co-parent. In fact, the parenting coordinator felt quite proud of his accomplishment until Marco remarked, "That doesn't mean anything. So what if she gave in twice. I have documented pages of her controlling behavior."

Are Marco and Anita still emotionally married? Their behavior toward each other would strongly suggest they are because like many couples who remain involved with each other after divorce, their attitudes and feelings lead to arguments, bitterness, and ongoing conflicts. For many such co-parenting couples, conflict may be expressed in hostility, anger, bitterness, revenge, and a general inability to deal with each other in a civilized, nonemotional way.

You may still be emotionally married if you have so much involvement with your co-parent and his or her personal business that you might as well still be living together.

> Although Terry and Krystie have been divorced for more than three years, he still has a key to her house and walks in without knocking. They take their children to church together on Sundays, and Krystie advises Terry on

the women he's dating. They have clearly not established the boundaries most divorced couples soon establish.

What about your boundaries with your co-parent? Do you know where that healthy line is between cooperation and intimacy? Do you think that your anger, fights, and conflict show that you have made a break from a close relationship with your ex?

If you are confused about the boundaries and acceptable behavior in your postdivorce relationship, you may still be emotionally married. When you remain emotionally married, the atmosphere is ideal for a high-conflict divorce.

Are You Still Emotionally Married?

To get a better sense of whether you're emotionally married to your ex-spouse, take this short quiz.

Check the box that best answers each question below:

1. Do I react to him or her in the same ways as I have for a long time when he or she annoys, irritates, or angers me or turns me on?

　　　　　　　□ Yes　□ No

2. Do I feel as angry now as when I got divorced?

　　　　　　　□ Yes　□ No

3. Have I established any new, essentially neutral ways of responding to his or her upsetting or attractive behaviors?

　　　　　　　□ Yes　□ No

4. Have I gotten over the hurt, anger, or sense of betrayal I initially felt?

　　　　　　　□ Yes　□ No

5. Do my co-parent and I have a pattern of behavior toward each other that is not working?

　　　　　　　□ Yes　□ No

(Continued)

Check the box . . . *(Continued)*

6. Do I still feel greatly drawn to my co-parent either sexually or for emotional comfort?

☐ Yes   ☐ No

7. Do I spend too much time thinking about my ex?

☐ Yes   ☐ No

8. Am I sometimes (or frequently) too involved in my co-parent's personal life?

☐ Yes   ☐ No

9. Do I get upset hearing what a good time the children had with my co-parent?

☐ Yes   ☐ No

10. Do I accept from or give to my co-parent excessive amounts of physical or financial assistance?

☐ Yes   ☐ No

If you answered yes to even one of these questions, you should seriously consider that you may continue to be emotionally married to your ex. If you answered yes to more than one, there is little doubt that you and your co-parent continue to have an emotional relationship that keeps one or both of you from truly moving on with your lives. Being emotionally married doesn't necessarily mean you have a high-conflict postdivorce relationship, but the chances are good that you are not moving on because you continue to be too attached to your former spouse.

Getting Married

When first getting married, most individuals have what would seem to be a true emotional marriage. There is a strong sense of love, commitment, and devotion — often expressed publicly in a marriage ceremony. Your world centers on your new partner. The feelings of love and loyalty are fierce, and the passion is strong.

And that's the way it should be in a marriage based on romantic love. All of the early feelings may last for years. However, the process of living — which often involves having children, advancing in careers, acquiring new friends, buying a house, and an assortment of other complications — will frequently intrude on the love, commitment, communication, and passion. With these complex aspects of life come distance, conflicts, arguments, and sometimes difficult-to-resolve issues that may lead to a cooling of the initial passion.

Divorce and Resolution

Couples who are not able to solve their problems and learn to communicate about the issues that inevitably occur in marriage may find themselves in divorce court. But by that time, you may be so angry with each other that letting go is relatively easy. It doesn't mean that the anger, sense of betrayal, resentment, or displeasure with one another will go away by the time a judge declares the marriage over. In fact, it usually takes most people (some experts estimate 80 percent) from one to two years to resolve their feelings and be able to work together in a fairly amicable atmosphere of cooperation for the sake of the children (King & Heard, 1999). These divorced individuals are able to move on with other relationships while continuing to be able to deal with their ex-spouse about the issues that parents must continually face.

For a minority of divorced couples with children — as many as twenty percent — moving on is not so easy (Buchanan & Heiges, 2001). These are the couples who are most likely still emotionally married and are often labeled as having a high-conflict divorce. Their resentment, their anger, their bitterness, and their inability to deal with each other in an unemotional, business-like way doom them to ongoing conflicts. These twenty percent are the people for whom this book is written. If you and your ex-spouse are in this group, you need extra help to learn to get along with each other and to sever the ties that keep you bound together in an emotional relationship for which there seems to be no end. This book will also help you if you are recently divorced and still traversing those difficult initial two years and would like to move beyond the early conflict much more quickly.

Quick Review

By about two years after their divorce, most couples will have resolved their feelings and begun to work together in a fairly amicable atmosphere of cooperation for the sake of the children. If you are still fighting with your ex-spouse and if your conflicts make you just as angry as before the divorce, you may still be emotionally married, that is, you may still have strong feelings for each other. If you and your ex-spouse are still emotionally married, you need extra help to learn to get along and to sever the ties that keep you bound.

CHAPTER 2

What Keeps the Conflict Alive?

When outsiders view a high-conflict divorce, they frequently ask, "Why do they keep on fighting with each other? Don't they know they're just hurting their kids?" Or they may wonder, "I don't know why they have so much trouble getting along. The marriage is over and yet neither of them can really let go of the past."

It's easy to take this objective, dispassionate point of view when you're standing on the outside looking in at other people's lives. Anyone can take a judgmental stance and say, "I don't get it. They hate each other so much. Why don't they think of what's best for their children and start getting along with each other?"

Indeed, that's a valid question — one that those of us who work constantly with high-conflict divorce relationships wonder ourselves. There has been some research on the subject, but it's not nearly satisfying. Nor do these studies explain a significant number of high-conflict divorces. Most of us in this field are still looking for a theory to explain a lot of high-conflict situations and to answer more questions than it generates.

> Gerard and Rita met in college, where she was a marketing major and he was a premed student. They fell in love and married, and Rita went to work for a marketing firm while Gerard attended medical school. It was a struggle to afford the expense of medical school. However, they were working together toward the same goal: for Gerard to one day be a surgeon in a large hospital. They both knew that all their early sacrifices would pay off.
>
> While Gerard was in his surgery residency, their first child was born. The second child was born when Gerard was in the midst of a surgery fellowship. After eight years of marriage and two children, Gerard and Rita were nearing the end of their hard work and could see an end to the financial hardships they had long endured.

Rita then discovered that Gerard was having an affair with a resident at the hospital. She was livid, felt betrayed, and filed for a divorce. Gerard, however, said he didn't want the marriage to end and apologized several times for his unfaithful behavior. Rita, though, was adamant. She said he had betrayed her trust and pressed forward with the divorce.

She said often that she couldn't forgive him and that she would "make him pay" for what he had done to her.

After the divorce, Rita tried to make life miserable for Gerard. He still loved her, though, and stalked her to learn more about her life and her activities. What they were doing to each other led to frequent motions and appearances in court, personal protection orders, and attempts to block access to the children.

In trying to figure out why co-parenting couples like Rita and Gerard have such a conflicted relationship, further questions must be asked: Why do some couples get both a legal divorce and an emotional divorce at pretty much the same time? And why do other couples remain emotionally married long after the legal divorce is over? In this chapter, we explain why you might be one of those twenty percenters — the one-fifth of divorced couples who have a high-conflict relationship.

The Factors Keeping People Emotionally Married

Various relationship factors, personality traits, and other psychological factors, emotions, personal histories, and even adversarial court processes seem to make some people more prone to remaining emotionally married. Let's look first at the most commonly involved relationship factors.

Relationship Factors Predicting High-Conflict Relationships

Our research and experience suggest that personality traits and various circumstances come together to contribute to four factors that are important in predicting ongoing hostility in postdivorce relationships:

1. Inability to agree with your co-parent
2. Inability to communicate with your co-parent
3. Inability to resolve issues with your co-parent without court intervention

4. Inability to show an interest in your children's well-being through interactions with your co-parent

These four factors are more important than others you might think play a part in the hostility and conflict between divorced couples, for instance, how much you are willing or able to spend (on lawyer's fees, for example) to get what you want. And these factors are probably more important than how much you love your children. Of course, most co-parents report loving their children and claim they have the ability to put their children's needs first. Despite that, in practice, individuals caught up in a high-conflict relationship have great difficulty putting their children's welfare ahead of their own feelings and anger.

Personality Traits and Psychological Factors That Lead to Co-Parent Conflict

There are some personality traits that in our opinion — and based on our years of clinical experience — lead some co-parenting couples to be unable to agree with one another, communicate, or avoid returns to court to settle issues and disputes.

Those traits that make people more prone to postdivorce fighting are

- A need for control
- Rigidity
- Insensitivity

A need for control. Everyone has a need for control in his or her life to a certain extent. However, when the need is excessive and extends to wanting to control others, including your co-parent, it becomes a negative trait that leads to conflict.

> Michael, a second-generation police officer, was described by his co-parent as a "control freak." Margaret said that Michael needed to control others in all sorts of ways. He needed to know what his children were doing every day, and he had a set of family rules that he tried to enforce on Margaret and the children even though he and Margaret were divorced and she had physical custody of the children. He called her daily to tell her when to take their children to the doctor or dentist, when she ought to talk to their teachers, and what they should wear to various events. He tried to control Margaret's life in the same way. He wanted to know who she dated, and he did background checks on people she went out with.

Margaret suspected that he sent patrol cars to her neighborhood to keep watch on her and the children.

Although the controlling person can appear to be organized, protective, and in charge of things, this personality trait becomes a detriment in interpersonal relationships — especially after a divorce. The co-parent of a controlling individual becomes very resentful and no longer views the attempts to exercise control as protection but as interference — which it is.

Rigidity. Leading to the inability to forgive and forget is the personality characteristic of rigidity. Recall Rita, who could not forgive a repentant Gerard for his affair; she typifies the rigid personality. Although such people can be structured, organized, and able to provide consistency — which are admirable qualities in a parent — they lack the flexibility to allow changes in relationships, failures in their co-parent, or deviation from a planned and structured approach to life.

Rita could work hard, care for her children and husband, and provide a consistent life for her children. But she couldn't understand or tolerate what she regarded as Gerard's moral lapse. No amount of apologizing on his part could lead to forgiveness. While forgiveness does not mean you condone your co-parent's behavior or that you will reconcile, forgiveness is important in reducing anger, freeing up your mind, and — with the stumbling block of indignation removed — helping you communicate more effectively.

After a divorce, the rigid individual will have difficulty making even minor adjustments to the schedule and may be very distressed at a co-parent who is five minutes late or does not get the kids exactly at bedtime.

Insensitivity.

Gregory came across as sensitive and caring. This was exactly what Desiree wanted in a man. She knew that someone as loving, caring, and concerned with her needs had to be the right person for her. She loved Gregory, and they got married. And when they had children, he seemed to care about the children's needs and feelings as well. Desiree could always rely on Gregory being sensitive.

After six years of marriage, Desiree began to view what she had previously regarded as his strength in a new light. "Of course, he's always sensitive when it doesn't matter," Desiree said. "However, if it's going to inconvenience him, he stops being so caring and so sensitive. In fact, at those times I wonder why I ever thought he was Mr. Sensitivity."

After the divorce, which Desiree initiated and Gregory resisted, he became even more insensitive to her. "Of course I care about her and the kids," he told people who knew them both. "But she doesn't care about me; why should I show her any consideration?"

When he wanted to have the children for parenting time or overnight visits, Gregory demanded his rights no matter what.

"I had plans for this weekend, because according to our schedule this was my weekend," Desiree would point out.

"I don't care," Gregory would say. "I've got an opportunity to take the kids to a baseball game. You should change your plans rather than denying them the chance to go to a great game!"

On other occasions, he would demand that because it was his weekend with the children, he didn't care if one of them was ill. "It's my weekend and I'm taking them!" Gregory would say. And other times he would let Desiree know at the last minute that a business trip "just came up" and he had to be out of town. "I expect you to switch your plans so I can make up the time by taking the kids next week."

Gregory is typical of the co-parent who seems to be very insensitive to the feelings and needs of his co-parent — and even his children. Such an individual professes interest in the feelings and needs of his co-parent and his children. However, his actions seem to say something quite different. He shows little ability to empathize with the other person.

In addition to the interpersonal factors that contribute to high-conflict postdivorce relationships, there are other personality factors that play a role in leading individuals to remain emotionally married. However, there is a limited amount of research that looks at these traits and the resulting degree of conflict. There's some evidence that individuals who have a defensive personality style are more likely to have a high-conflict divorce (Ackerman, 1995; Postuma & Harper, 1998; Siegel, 1996; Siegel & Langford, 1998). Some studies have suggested that narcissistic qualities lead to difficulties, especially during child custody conflicts between divorced parents (Johnston & Campbell, 1988). Narcissistic parents are more concerned with their own well-being than with the well-being of their children.

Emotions That Can Be Predictors

Conflict often results from the anger, bitterness, resentment, or other feelings that are the aftermath of divorce. Based on our experience with couples in high conflict, we have concluded that the emotions that come about during and after divorce are likely to interfere with your ability to process the grief resulting from your divorce. During and after a divorce, many people find anger easier to tolerate than sadness, which may feel frightening and overwhelming. Friends and family may also feel more comfortable dealing with an angry divorced person than a depressed one and so may encourage anger but not grief.

It is also fairly common after a marriage ends because of unfaithfulness to become fixated on the affair as the reason for all problems despite the many unhappy years before that. The "injured" co-parent may feel betrayed, abandoned, or misused. Or she may have deep-seated feelings of betrayal that result in anger, sadness, and even thoughts of revenge.

Personal Histories Play a Role in Conflict Too

What you have experienced in your life may play a distinct role in whether you engage in intense conflict following a divorce.

> For example, Karen's parents divorced when she was nine. After the divorce, her parents fought constantly, and her father was abusive to her mother. Her father was also an alcoholic who spent little time with Karen after she turned twelve.
>
> When Karen was a teenager, she vowed that she would marry someone who was not like her father, and, furthermore, she wanted her marriage to last forever. Most of all, she wanted a husband who enjoyed their children and was family oriented.
>
> Karen was sure she found the right man in Dajuan. He seemed to be everything her father wasn't. He loved children, was close to his own family, and didn't drink. Karen was convinced that her marriage to Dajuan would be completely different from her parents' marriage. However, seven years into the marriage, Dajuan began drinking and when he was physically abusive to their two children, Karen felt she had no choice but to leave him. However, she felt betrayed and angrily blamed Dajuan for ruining her dreams for a family life she didn't have as a child.

When a marriage — and a subsequent divorce — stirs up emotions from childhood, the resulting feelings can lead to intense hurt, which can consequently lead to a high-conflict relationship.

The Adversarial Divorce Process

An adversarial divorce process can set the stage for postdivorce conflict. For instance, if a divorce attorney encourages or condones such activities as videotaping the co-parent or the children, taping phone conversations, threatening to take the children, or threatening to ruin the co-parent financially, these actions may inflame insecurities, heighten mistrust, and increase hostility. On the other hand, a cooperative divorce can diminish fears, reduce anxiety, and help maintain respect between co-parents, thus making it easier for both individuals to deal with their grief.

Putting It All Together

We said at the beginning of this chapter that we would offer an explanation to help you better understand why you might be one of those twenty percenters — the one-fifth of divorced couples who have a high-conflict relationship.

As we have said, there is no one theory that ties together the aspects that contribute to a high-conflict postdivorce relationship, but there are several significant factors that relate to why some couples are more prone to remaining emotionally married. Based on primary research, the current professional literature, and our years of clinical experience, the multiple factors influencing the possibility of experiencing a contentious divorce are personality factors, co-parent interactions, emotions, personal histories, and an adversarial court process.

As we mentioned, our observations and research suggest that four factors seem to play a significant role in whether you end up with a high-conflict relationship: the ability of you and your co-parent to agree with each other, your overall ability to communicate with each other, your willingness to resolve issues together, and your belief that your co-parent is interacting with you in a way that benefits your child. Although these ideas seem ridiculously simple, they are likely affected by the other factors — your personality, your personal history, and the depth of your negative emotions — more than you might imagine.

In other words, if you could talk to one another and frequently found yourself in agreement with each other before you began having problems in your marriage, the chances are much less that you would be in a high-conflict relationship later — or if you were, it wouldn't last long.

We've observed that many high-conflict divorce couples who confessed that they never got along very well often had the most intense and angry conflicts. Conversely, those who said that they were always able to talk with each other and were usually in agreement about such things as finances and discipline of the children were much better able to work through their conflicts and stop the battles between each other.

Quick Review

Various relationship factors — personality traits and other psychological factors, emotions, personal histories, and even adversarial court processes — make some people more prone to remaining emotionally married.

Personality traits that lead to poor co-parent relationships include a need for control, rigidity, and insensitivity. What you have experienced in your life also plays a distinct role in whether you engage in intense conflict following a divorce. An adversarial divorce process can set the stage for postdivorce conflict as well.

These factors play a role in postdivorce conflict, but the reason you or someone you know is in a high-conflict relationship may either be a combination of the factors discussed in this chapter or be quite unique.

Strategies to Change Yourself

CHAPTER 3

What Is Your Goal?

People get divorced in order to change something in their lives. Alvin got a divorce to get away from the conflict he had with his wife. Phyllis got a divorce to get away from the negativity she encountered with her husband. Nicholas left his long-time partner so he could change his career. Stacey obtained a divorce so she could have a greater sense of control over her life. Jeremy's main motivation for a divorce was to pursue a relationship with a woman he considered the love of his life.

Whether it's to move to another state, get away from an abusive partner, leave a loveless relationship, or get away from an alcoholic spouse, everyone gets a divorce for some reason. The goals you have leading to a divorce may seem laudable or silly to others. To you, though, your goals are very important.

Goals in a Contentious Relationship

Although following a divorce some individuals lose sight of the goals that motivated their divorce, others become very narrowly focused when they remain emotionally married. If your goals are narrowly focused — to get even with your co-parent or to get full custody of the children — you are likely to lose sight of other very important parts of your life.

And if you remain frustrated and angry with your co-parent, energy is being taken away from the pleasures of daily life and the connection you have with those who currently are the significant others in your life. If you're not having fun because you're too focused on your anger or resentment toward your former spouse, then your positive and potentially productive goals have been lost.

> Take that energy you've been using up to get back at
> your co-parent and put it to use in CREATING a new
> life rather than fighting the old one you had.

Focus Your Goals on Creating a New You

A divorce is a crisis, and you can either use a crisis for growth or allow it to cause stagnation. Why not use it for your own growth? You are now free to develop new passions, hobbies, career goals, and greatly improved relationships with your children or other people in your life. What a shame if you let the anger, resentment, or bitterness toward your co-parent keep you mired in an emotional marriage filled with conflict.

Questions to Ask Yourself

Because you are facing an opportunity to change your life, here are some questions you should ask yourself:

- What do I want to do differently with my life and freedom?
- What have I always loved or wished to do?
- What is important to me?
- What do I need to work on? My job skills? My public speaking? My time spent with friends and family?
- When I was married, what did I give up?
- What did I blame my co-parent for stopping me from doing?
- If I could create the perfect life for myself now, what would it look like?
- Where do I want to be in five years? In ten years?
- What little things can I do daily to enjoy life?
- What kind of relationship do I want to have with my children?
- How can I handle this divorce in a way that is consistent with the kind of person I am or want to be?

- What would make my life more meaningful?
- Do I need to reconnect with any relationships from which I have been cut off?

Steps to Focus Your Goals

Research in goal setting and task motivation over the past forty years has shown people are more successful when they are committed to their goals (Hollenbeck, Williams, & Klein, 1989). Furthermore, commitment is stronger when goals are difficult (Klein, Wesson, Hollenbeck, & Alge, 1999). Making a public commitment to your goals and writing your goals down are essential parts of reaching them successfully (Locke & Latham, 2002). Mental practice and rehearsal have also been found to be significant in the achievement of goals (Richardson, 1967). Therefore, the following steps to focus and commit to your goals are very important.

Step 1. Brainstorm your hopes and dreams. Find a quiet time and quiet and comfortable surroundings. In a journal or on a pad of paper, spend fifteen to thirty minutes answering the above questions and writing down new possibilities for life involving your career, hobbies, passions, purpose, and even retirement. Do not rule anything out. Do not censor yourself with comments such as "I'm too old to go to medical school" or "I don't have enough money, time, or energy to start a manufacturing company." Everything that seems interesting or has been a hope, a dream, or a direction gets written down.

Step 2. Visualize yourself in situations that represent a dream for you. Take ten to fifteen minutes a day to visualize yourself, for instance, going to law school or starting a new company. Visualize every detail from what you are wearing, to how you feel, to how you carry yourself. See yourself interacting with the people you would encounter or giving a presentation about the new direction of your life. Imagine how it will feel when you are successful.

Step 3. Make a list of concrete goals and action steps you could take to reach your goal. After you have spent time visualizing your new pathways, you may find that you have been drawn to one or more of them. It is now time to write down your goals for personal growth, health and fitness, career, family, or the future. Don't overwhelm yourself with too many goals, nor make your goals either too easy or too difficult. Keep them simple, but at the same time make sure there's a balance between difficulty and achievability.

For example, if your goal is to become more physically fit, your concrete goals might be the following:

- I will exercise by walking thirty minutes a day.
- I will play tennis three times a week.
- I will design a diet with my doctor or personal trainer.
- I will go to the gym three times a week and work with a personal trainer.

Or if your goal is to get that accounting degree you started before you got married, you might have these practical goals:

- Go on the Internet and look at program options.
- Call colleges to find out about costs and financial aid.
- Select the college and program you'd like to attend.
- Meet with an advisor to work out a schedule.
- Talk to your boss to see if you could take courses and time off if needed to attend classes that meet during your scheduled work time.

Susie had given up the piano after getting married and having three children. Now she was divorced, working a full-time job, and caring for her children after work, but one of the things she missed was her piano. Her goal was to go back to playing the piano because she recognized that it provided her joy before and she still thought she could be a skilled piano player.

She thought about how nice it would be to play and sing with the kids and with friends. After exploring this goal and deciding she wanted to pursue it, she met a woman who was a retired music teacher who was flexible with her time and charges. Susie arranged to take lessons with her and she started playing again. She began practicing after the children were asleep at night, and she found that when she practiced she was totally absorbed in her playing. That helped her forget about the stress of the divorce. In fact, the conflict with her co-parent took on less importance as she focused more on what she could accomplish with her music than what she lost in the marriage.

Your goal might be aimed more at personal improvement, such as being a more positive person. The steps you could take to be that more positive person could be:

Step 1. Write down positive things in your life or your positive qualities.
Step 2. Review your list every morning.
Step 3. Smile more often.
Step 4. Talk yourself out of negative thoughts or substitute positive thoughts for negative thoughts.

Establish Limited Goals

In our work with high-conflict divorce couples, we've learned that if your goals are too lofty, you're likely to fail or at least feel frustrated. It's better to establish more limited goals.

Why start out with the goal of solving *all* your problems or living *all* your dreams, when it's a lot more practical to set up a few limited goals? You could decide to try to solve two conflicts with your co-parent. Or, like Susie, to focus on the goal of playing the piano again. Or, like Vincente, of finishing college and getting the B.A. he always wanted to have. If you accomplish your limited goals, you can then establish new ones.

> Geoff had always wanted to write a book. When he got married and became a father, that dream was sidetracked as he devoted his energies to supporting his family.
>
> After his marriage to Jillian ended in divorce, Geoff was preoccupied with new issues — parenting time concerns, paying child support, and battles with Jillian over his role as a father.
>
> One day, about two years after the marriage ended, Geoff began to think about the goal he had deferred. "I've been so busy fighting with Jillian that I haven't been thinking about writing that book," he thought. "Maybe now is the perfect time. I've had enough experiences and I have a much clearer idea of the book I want to write. This book could be incorporated into my other ideas for a new direction in my life." Geoff spent several days thinking about his book and how it could lead to marketing himself as a business consultant.

However, he knew he couldn't just quit his job and start writing. The more realistic goal, he thought to himself, would be to set aside about ten hours a week to do research. Then, after six months of research, he could start writing. He could use vacation time he accumulated to be away from his job and really concentrate on writing. With that limited but achievable goal firmly in place, Geoffrey set a date for starting the research that would eventually result in a completed book.

It's often a setup for failure to try to tackle your most intense or most contentious issue first. Instead, choose an easier conflict to take on initially. You're more likely to be successful with an easier goal, say a resolvable conflict, than with the most difficult one. When you are flushed with good feelings based on your initial success, go on to a slightly more difficult one.

Kurt and Natalie had been fighting for a year over the use of medication for their ten-year-old son, Devon, who was diagnosed with attention deficit hyperactivity disorder. Natalie believed it was essential that Devon take his Concerta daily. Kurt didn't agree with the diagnosis of ADHD and certainly didn't want his son taking any medication.

Kurt and Natalie battled over this issue for months without reaching an agreement. However, because Natalie had physical custody, she got a prescription for Concerta from a psychiatrist. Yet, when Devon spent time at Kurt's house, Kurt refused to give him the medication. This infuriated Natalie, and the inconsistency was unhealthy for Devon.

Whether Devon had ADHD or whether he would take medication for this condition were not the only conflicts Natalie and Kurt had with each other. They couldn't agree on discipline approaches any easier than on the ADHD medication. They did agree that they'd always had trouble communicating, and they agreed that communication was perhaps the underlying conflict between them.

When it came to trying to work out some of the issues that kept them so angry with each other, they decided that it would be foolhardy to select the conflict over the ADHD medication as the first problem they would try to solve. It made much more sense to take on the more general issue of communication.

As it turned out, when they each brainstormed some ideas for solving their problems with communication, they came up with good ideas. Among them were:

- We should set up a regular time to talk on the phone and share information about our son.

- We should let each other know ahead of time about doctor and dentist appointments or school conferences.
- We should email each other each week to indicate the things we want to talk about when we have our next phone conversation.
- We should treat each other with respect whenever we talk on the phone.

They agreed that these were excellent ideas. They wrote them out in an agreement and both signed the agreement. This initial success made them both feel positive about taking on a slightly more challenging concern. The second one they chose to work on had to do with their son playing sports. They knew they were still not ready to take on the problem of the ADHD medication. But they could see that with more successes, they might be able to get there. That feeling of making progress in talking to each other was a new one for both of them.

Quick Review

If you're stuck in an emotional relationship with your co-parent after a divorce, you may be missing out on opportunities to start anew.

Think about the golden opportunity you have for exploring your dreams and goals. Reflect on your goals and establish some practical goals for yourself.

Set limited goals, but write down practical steps and action plans so you will be successful in reaching your initial goals.

When you have reached your first goals, go on to more difficult ones.

But remember: focus on your dreams and goals rather than on the anger you have toward your co-parent.

CHAPTER 4

Identifying Your Emotional Hot Buttons

Everyone has "hot buttons." It's like there's a panel inside us with a number of lighted buttons. If someone pushes one of these buttons, our anger alarm goes off.

Darius had his hot buttons. All it took to set off his anger alarm was for his co-parent, Rebecca, to bring the kids back a few minutes late. Another one of his hot buttons was if Rebecca asked to switch weekends. "What!" Darius would roar into the phone. "The court order says that's my weekend and I'm not switching!"

Whitney had her hot buttons as well. "I'm a pretty easygoing person normally," she says, "but if Sidney tries to tell me how to discipline the kids, I go ballistic. I know I have a problem with my anger around him, but he just sets me off. It's not rational, but that's the way I react to him and his criticizing how I discipline the children."

Sam certainly had his hot buttons when it came to Lauren. "I know I was jealous when we were married," Sam says, "but my feelings haven't gone away since we got divorced. I know she's entitled to go on with her life, but I just get enraged when I even hear that she's dating another man."

When five-year-old Hank told Sam that a man was at Lauren's house when Hank was there, Sam demanded to know who the man was and if he spent the night. "You have no right exposing our son to a strange man!" Sam yelled at Lauren. "If Hank tells me again about a man being at your house when he's there, I'll have you back in front of the judge and I'll file child abuse charges against you!"

If you want to get control over your emotions, especially your anger, the first step is to identify your emotional hot buttons.

What Exactly Are Emotional Hot Buttons?

Emotional hot buttons are your anger triggers. Everyone has different anger triggers, but we all have them. And for the most part, they are normal and reasonable. However, given the history you have with your co-parent, your particular emotional hot buttons will be based on past hurts, disappointments, resentments, betrayals, frustrations, and so on. Your triggers may be perfectly reasonable — or they may be irrational or not easily understood by anyone else.

Darius gets so angry when his co-parent is late picking up the children; if she's even a few minutes late, Darius is livid. Other people, given the same situation, would react with more understanding and acceptance. In fact, Darius's brother says, "If it was me, I'd just say, 'Okay, try to be on time next time' and I'd let it go." But, for whatever reasons, Darius can't do that.

Similarly, Whitney's anger over her co-parent's attempts to tell her how to discipline their children makes her crazy with anger. Her best friend can't understand Whitney's reactions. "My ex always criticizes how I'm raising the kids, but I just shrug it off," the friend says. "I know I'm doing a good job, so I just forget about it."

It is important to identify all of your emotional hot buttons in order to begin doing something about them.

Identify Your Emotional Hot Buttons

As an exercise, make a list of all your hot buttons that your co-parent pushes. Find out how many you have.

You've Identified Your Hot Buttons. What Now?

Once you have a list of them, decide which ones are rational and reasonable, and decide which ones are anything but reasonable and rational. Which ones make you crazy? To which hot buttons do you overreact? These are the super hot buttons — and these are the anger triggers you need to work on.

Defusing Your Hot Buttons

The next step is to begin to defuse the intense anger triggered when your super hot buttons are pushed. Here are the steps to defusing your most sensitive hot buttons:

1. Visualize your co-parent pushing one of those hot buttons.
2. Take three slow, deep breaths as you think about her pushing one of your hot buttons by, for instance, coming late to pick up the kids.
3. Tell yourself that it is not worth it to get upset about this.
4. Continue to breathe in a deep, relaxing way.
5. Practice this exercise over and over until you can visualize this situation without getting angry.

Learn More about Anger Management

The next chapter discusses various ways you can use anger management techniques to better control your anger. Learn as much as you can about anger management and recognize that you won't get better at defusing the anger associated with your emotional hot buttons unless you practice anger management.

Quick Review

Everyone has emotional hot buttons — those buttons your co-parent pushes that make you so angry. In order to defuse these anger triggers, you must first identify them. Next you have to practice visualizing the trigger being set off by your co-parent. Then, while visualizing this, practice taking slow, deep breaths. Do this until you are feeling calmer and more relaxed.

Read the next chapter to learn more about anger management.

CHAPTER 5

Letting Go of Your Anger

Of course you're angry. Who wouldn't be? After all, consider everything that has happened since it became clear your marriage wouldn't work. *She* was having an affair. *He* betrayed you. *She* tried to use the children to get back at you. *He* had more money to spend on lawyers, and look at the shark *he* hired. *She* tried to get you fired from your job. *He* began dating your best friend. *She* took you to court over the smallest things.

You have every reason to be angry. However, when the anger goes on for an extended period of time and gets in the way of getting on with your life or is affecting the mental health of your children, it's time to say, "Enough's enough!" Or perhaps you've said to yourself, "Get over it!" Maybe even your closest friend has already told you that. Or maybe you just decided that on your own. Maybe you're simply worn out from being mad all the time. And maybe you really would like to get on with your life without that awful burden of anger.

Whatever the reason, you know you need to stop feeling so angry. In many ways, that's what this whole book is about, and in this chapter we're going to give you some practical steps you can use for getting over your anger and moving on.

But How Do You Let Go of Your Anger?

One way to get there is to acknowledge your anger. Admit it, talk about it, and then set it aside. It always sounds easy when the prescription is written in such simple terms. However, the human brain and our emotions are far from simple. It's often as if our feelings have a life of their own. Intellectually, you can say you accept that he had an affair and you forgive him. However, that's when the emotions step in and say,

"Wait a minute! You're taking this affront to your marriage and your respect in a very cavalier manner. What about the betrayal? The trust you had in him? Your dreams about growing old together? How can you just say you forgive him? We don't forgive him — and maybe we never will!"

Okay, so it's not so easy to set aside those emotions and stop feeling angry. Here are some ways to stop feeling so angry.

Three Steps for Letting Your Anger Go

1. Stop worshipping your anger.
2. Forgive your co-parent.
3. Use anger management techniques daily.

---

1. Stop Worshipping Your Anger

If you're holding on to your anger longer than you ever thought possible, you're worshipping that anger. What do we mean by this? Let's look at Michelle as an example of an individual worshipping her anger.

Michelle was married for six years to Jack, a man she met when she was in her early twenties. They dated for a year and got married, even though she knew that he enjoyed gambling and that he drank much more than she did. However, Michelle rationalized that he had a good job, wanted to have children, and seemed to adore her.

In the six years of their marriage, they had three children, but during those years, Jack's gambling became more of an addiction and he was drinking to get drunk much more often. When she discovered that he was using the money meant for the mortgage and the car payment to gamble, she became concerned enough to take over the family finances. However, he used credit cards she didn't know about to continue to gamble, and as his losses mounted, so did his secret credit card debt along with the amount he was drinking.

When Jack was arrested for driving under the influence of alcohol and leaving the scene of an accident, he was jailed for sixty days. During that time, she learned about his credit card debt, which approached nearly $100,000. When he was released from jail, she confronted him about his gambling and his drinking. He denied that he had a problem with either his drinking or his gambling, and Michelle was concerned that he would destroy the family if she remained married to him. She filed for divorce, and he did not protest her actions.

She was stuck with some of the debt and had to take on a second job to try to repay the credit cards and support herself and the children. Jack did everything he could to make her life miserable. He blamed her for his drinking. He said she was too controlling and accused her of turning the children against him. Somehow he found an attorney who filed a motion for Jack to have full custody of the children. It cost Michelle more money to fight this, and although he didn't get custody of the children, he did retain weekend parenting time with them.

Michelle was angry about the divorce, Jack's gambling and drinking, and the disgrace he brought to her. After the divorce, he gave her even more reasons to be angry when she learned that he was often intoxicated when he picked up the kids on Friday nights and that he frequently was impaired when he drove with the children in the car. Michelle sought help from the court, but she felt like all she got was the runaround. The judge refused to limit his parenting time or to order him to get treatment for his alcoholism. Michelle was angry and afraid that he would hurt the children or even kill them in a car accident.

Michelle regularly wrote letters to the court, filed motions with the court, and talked to whoever would listen about Jack and his irresponsible behavior. She felt like no one listened to her or believed her. As she felt she was not taken seriously, she got angrier and more strident in her efforts to get some help. Once in a court hearing, she screamed at the judge, "What do you care if he kills our children! You're on his side and you can write me off as a crazy, angry person!" That got her a contempt citation, but it didn't do anything but increase her anger. Now she was mad at Jack and at "the system."

When she talked to the court social worker, she alternately cried and screamed. No one wanted to talk with her because she appeared to be an irrational person who accused everyone of being part of the unjust system that made her life "a living hell."

Michelle had many reasons to be angry. But her anger became the central focus of her life. One of her therapists wondered what she would do if she stopped being angry. "She seems to live for her anger," the therapist said.

When your anger becomes the greatest motivating force in your life, when you almost need to be angry every day in order to carry on a crusade for justice, when your life revolves around your anger, you are worshipping your anger. Your goal is not to rid yourself of your anger, although you may say this is so; rather your goal is to use the energy of the anger to win the justice you think you deserve. When people like Michelle worship their anger, they are not going to get over that anger and they are going to affect nearly everyone they come in contact in.

Ronald Potter-Efron, Ph.D. has said that there are six main reasons people hold on to their anger. Those reasons are (1) power and control, (2) giving away responsibility, (3) poor communication skills, (4) avoiding other feelings or people, (5) habit, and (6) the anger rush (Potter-Efron, 1994).

If you are angry too much of the time, one of these reasons may explain why. Michelle enjoyed the rush that she got daily from her anger.

2. When You Stop Worshipping Your Anger, You Are Free to Forgive Your Co-Parent

The first thing you can do to reduce your anger is to forgive your co-parent. Forgiving someone who has wronged you is very difficult — but it is also very powerful. In fact, we believe it is so important that chapter 7 is devoted to forgiveness. However, here it is important to see it as a step in anger reduction. It is almost impossible to forgive someone and at the same time be angry with him. This is what Emily discovered.

> Emily carried around her anger after she divorced Corey. During their marriage, he physically abused her daughter from a previous marriage. When his excessive spanking and slapping of her daughter came to light, she notified child protective services and filed for a divorce.
>
> "I couldn't accept that he could be so evil as to hurt my daughter," Emily said. "I wanted to see him go to prison."
>
> But Corey didn't go to prison. He was charged with child abuse, placed on probation, and forbidden to be alone with Emily's daughter. It was also ordered that he attend parenting classes and go to an anger management program as well as have supervised parenting time with the two children he shared with Emily. "I was so angry with him I couldn't even think about him being alone with our children, and I was prepared to fight him forever to keep him from having nonsupervised time with our kids."
>
> After fighting Corey in and out of the courts, Emily recognized that she was being consumed by her anger. Although she didn't trust Corey, she also saw that her anger was detrimental to her well-being. When

Corey successfully completed an anger management program and finished the parenting classes, he said that he had changed and understood better why he treated Emily's daughter so harshly and that he was sure he would never treat any other children, especially his own, as he did her daughter.

"My pastor recommended that I forgive him," Emily said. "At first I thought he was crazy. Then the more I thought about it, the more it seemed to be the best way to save myself. So I forgave him. I forgave him for being weak, for being so angry with my daughter, and for hurting her. Now, I don't need to be angry with him. Mostly, I just pity him for the way he was, and I'm trying to keep an open mind about him having changed."

Emily understood what is hard for other co-parents to come to see: that few people are deliberately or completely malevolent. Instead, people have complex reasons that account for their "bad" behavior. More importantly, she understood that continuing to be angry with him served no purpose — for her, for him, or for her children.

3. Taking Actions to Reduce Your Anger

You can do something about your anger — when you're ready. Sometimes it takes co-parents a few months, sometimes even a couple of years, to be ready to do something about the corroding effects of their anger.

It may be helpful to know how other people have gotten ready to stop idolizing their anger and prepare themselves for a change.

Ramone said he got a wake-up call when his eight-year-old daughter said to him, "Dad, why are you always mad at me?" "That hit me like a slap in the face," Ramone said. "I never realized that my darling daughter thought I was mad at her. I was mad at her mother, but she thought I was mad at her. I knew right then I had to do something."

Carolyn realized she had to do something about her anger when she was arguing with her co-parent, who had dropped off their nine-year-old son earlier. "We were talking in the kitchen and it turned into our usual argument and both of us were raising our voices," Carolyn recalled. "I thought our son was sound asleep in his room, and I never imagined he could hear us arguing. But he suddenly was standing in the doorway to the kitchen, and he was crying and he said, 'Please stop fighting; I'm scared.'"

Carolyn said that it stopped both her and her co-parent right in their tracks. "I never thought my anger and the arguments we were having were affecting our son," she said. "But they were, and I knew they had to stop."

Zach remembered the night after an argument with his co-parent when he found himself wondering how he should kill her. "That was a rude awakening," Zach said. "Here I was a law enforcement officer, and I was thinking of the worst possible crime. I had to get it under control or I'd end up in prison."

Other co-parents have told us that they knew they had to do something about their anger when they were experiencing physical symptoms related to stress or they overheard others referring to them as "grouchy," "bitchy," or "always angry."

Carolyn, Ramone, Zach, and other co-parents who had an epiphany about their anger recognized that they had to get it under control — or their anger would control them.

Use Anger Management Techniques to Control Your Reactions

Potter-Efron, a recognized anger expert, contends that people who are angry all the time need to climb down and get off the anger ladder because it is ruining their lives (Potter-Efron, 1994). He lists many rules for climbing down that ladder. Among them are the following:

- Take time out to stop your anger and violence.
- Wipe the frown off your face and relax.
- Quit trying to control others.
- Ask; don't demand.
- Speak quietly and don't swear.
- Be responsible for everything you say and do.
- Use "I" statements.

These rules are important ones to heed because they will lead you to relax more, help you control both your anger and violence, and help you show respect to the person with whom you are angry.

To help you climb down the anger ladder during interactions with your co-parent, you can use some or all of Potter-Efron's rules. In addition, you can utilize other proven anger management techniques to control your reactions.

**Three Important Anger Management Techniques to
Control Your Physical Reactions to Your Co-Parent**
- Count to ten.
- Take deep breaths.
- Relax your muscles.

Three useful methods of managing the physiological reactions to your anger with your co-parent are counting to ten, taking deep breaths, and using deep muscle relaxation. All three have been shown to be useful in dealing with anger — particularly the kind of reactions that are visceral: rapid breathing, increased blood pressure, tightness in your chest, a headache, stomach pains, or tightness in your muscles (DiGiuseppe and Tafrate, 2001).

Simply by counting slowly to ten, you can better control those physiological reactions that clearly show you are upset and angry. Also, taking a minimum of three deep breaths can calm your emotions and produce a more relaxed state. And, finally, deep muscle relaxation is a procedure that once learned can be used instantaneously to produce relaxation. You can go to one of the books or websites listed in the references and online resources sections to learn about progressive relaxation and other calming techniques.

These relaxation methods help you control yourself so you can interact or respond in a more relaxed manner. However, there are other methods that can be successfully used as you go into a confrontation or right after an encounter that has upset you.

Other anger management techniques are more thoughtful, such as:

- Self-talk
- Risk assessment
- Magic mantra
- Reframing

Your brain can be a powerful and capable ally should you choose to use it. Okay, so sometimes your emotions do take over, particularly if you've trained yourself to respond that way, but once you decide to find a solution to a problem you can get your brain in gear and use your thinking abilities productively. That's why these techniques, which are referred to as cognitive techniques (DiGiuseppe and Tafrate, 2001), will work for you.

Self-Talk

We all talk to ourselves, using silent speech constantly. Although when we're angry that silent speech can be fairly hostile and volatile ("I wish I'd never married the jerk! I'd like to ruin his life just like he's ruined mine!"), we can change that once we realize we have control over that part of us. That is, you can change your negative self-talk into positive self-talk. This is the way Ghassan did it.

> "The best way of getting back at her is to just keep filing motions in court," Ghassan said. "She can't afford to continue hiring an attorney to go back into court, so I'll file motions to request physical custody of our daughter. That will make her crazy, and she'll spend more money then she can afford fighting me.
>
> "But, what do I win if I keep this up? Okay, I can prove that I have more money to blow on attorneys than she does. And I guess I can prove that she will battle me in court if she thinks she could lose time with our daughter. But why exactly do I need to prove these things? And who will it hurt? I'm sure the person who will get hurt the most is our daughter. She didn't ask for us to treat each other so badly. And what will it teach her? To be mean and nasty to others? Is that what I want her to learn growing up? If I stop being so angry and vindictive against her mother, I hope our daughter will see me in a positive way and I'm sure she will love me more than if I actually ruined her mother financially."
>
> By talking it through in his head — a process that can take days, weeks, or even months — Ghassan changed his negative self-talk into positive self-talk and made an important decision for himself: he would rather influence his daughter in a positive way than a negative way. Whenever you catch yourself using negative self-talk, change it to positive self-talk.

Risk Assessment

By thinking about the downside of your anger, you can see that the risks may be greater than the benefits of expressing or even holding on to your anger. This thinking approach requires considering what the risks are and how it is often too risky to express your anger.

For example, Mary, who has a family history of heart disease, finally understood after several months of being angry with her co-parent for the way he handled the divorce that if she continued to feel angry, she would be contributing to her *own* heart problems. Miguel stopped stalking his co-parent when he realized that if she filed a complaint against him and he was charged with stalking he could lose his job and maybe even go to jail. And Kevin, who considered kidnapping his daughter in order to hurt his former wife, recognized that he would be hurting his daughter far more than he would hurt his co-parent by keeping them apart.

Magic Mantra

Creating or developing a magic mantra can come in handy when you experience instant anger. For example, if during the exchange of your children your co-parent indicates he'll be bringing the children back two hours late on Sunday night, you may find yourself instantaneously angry. After all, you already talked to him about the fact that the children need to be home on Sunday night at six o'clock to wind down, take baths, and get to bed early so they are ready for school when the alarm goes off on Monday morning. Inside, you're saying to yourself, "He's so inconsiderate of me and the children! He's doing this on purpose to make me mad! He's always trying to change the routine that's best for the kids!"

But if you listen to those angry thoughts, you're going to be shouting at him, and an argument will occur. That's where your magic mantra comes in. You could have a predetermined word or phrase that you say to yourself that will be your signal to chill out. In fact, that could be your magic mantra in these kinds of situations: "Chill out." Repeat this mantra in your head, and instead of focusing on what he is doing or saying to raise your blood pressure, focus on finding calmness.

Other mantras that co-parents use are "Calm down," "Take it easy," "Relax," and "Let it go." Find a magic mantra that works for you and say it to yourself — perhaps several times — until you have your anger under control or until you can use one of the other methods you've learned in this chapter. Try practicing this in other situations that typically anger you first, such as in heavy traffic, so that you can develop your response.

Reframing

Reframing is an important way to change how you think. It's a way of thinking in which you choose how you frame — or look at — a situation. For instance, you can think that your co-parent is attempting to control you or you can choose to think that she is just trying to do what is best for the children. You are likely to feel much less anger if you reframe how you think about her intentions.

How you frame your experiences influences how you feel. There are many frames for every situation, and you get to choose the frame you want. Choose a frame that casts your co-parent's behavior and actions in a way that suggests a deliberate attempt to make your life miserable, and inevitably you'll feel angry. Select a different frame, and you will feel something other than anger — perhaps pity, sadness, compassion, or even amusement!

Unfortunately, many co-parents use rigid frames. That is, the frames they select in looking at their co-parent are negative ones that they feel powerless to change. For example, the following quotes are instances in which co-parents framed their co-parent and their co-parent's actions in negative ways:

- "He's just trying to control me."
- "She's trying to turn the kids against me."
- "He doesn't want to agree on medication for our son because he doesn't care whether our son gets better or not."

But apply reframing to the same situations and you can look at them differently, often with less anger and fewer negative emotions. Here are ways of reframing negative situations to reduce or eliminate your anger:

- Your co-parent attempts to control your life: "Her problem is that she feels she has little or no control over most situations in her life, and her solution is to try to micromanage mine."
- Your co-parent says negative things about you to the children: "I think his attempts to turn the kids against me reflect how insecure he is. He's afraid that if he says good things about me,

the children will love me more than they love him. I feel sorry for him because he's so insecure, but I'm pretty confident that the children will love me no matter what he says about me."

- Your co-parent refuses to agree on the use of medication for your child: "She's fearful that if our son takes this medication it will harm him in some way. Maybe this is a blessing in disguise because she might agree on us finding alternative approaches to helping our son concentrate better at school."

If you have negative ways of thinking and you can't reframe your thoughts, you may be stuck in an anger rut. Reframe how you think about the situation, and you may well change how you react to your co-parent.

Do Something Positive to Deal with Your Anger

Not only can you use relaxation techniques and thinking techniques to control your anger, but you can also take active steps to deal with your anger. We all know that being active, engaging in vigorous movement and moving your muscles in daily exercise, can ward off depression and reduce stress. Being active can also work for anger reduction.

It is important to be active and get out and get moving every day. Not only will running a few miles, biking several miles, lifting weights for an hour, taking a dance class, or rowing a boat for an hour make you more physically fit, it will also help you deal with the anger demons in your life. It's hard to maintain intense anger after you've just worked out for an hour and those great endorphins are swimming around your body creating positive energy. In other words, substituting positive behaviors may work wonders as you try to better control your anger.

Apologize, Forgive, or Create an Emotional Divorce Ritual

Just as remaining angry has different causes for different people, it also has different solutions. Many find the methods we discuss in future chapters effective. The next chapter discusses apologizing, chapter 7 describes how to forgive, and chapter 10 is about creating a ritual — a personalized way to ritualize a major life event. Developing a personally designed anger ritual will help you stop worshipping your anger and get rid of it forever.

Quick Review

If you're stuck in an anger rut and can't get out of it, try using anger management techniques. Learn and practice counting to ten, taking deep breaths, or using muscle relaxation. Also, you can put some thinking procedures into practice. Self-talk, risk assessment, and reframing are all helpful in thinking your way to less anger. Finally, vigorous exercise and body movement can be especially helpful in releasing the endorphins that lead to increased feelings of well-being while decreasing the corrosive effects of anger.

CHAPTER 6

Apologies and How to Use Them

Lynn Johnston (of the comic strip "For Better or For Worse") once said that "an apology is the superglue of life; it can repair just about anything." There's a lot of truth in that. It's amazing how far an apology goes in healing hurts and wounds. Perhaps an apology could help heal the rift between you and your co-parent. We aren't suggesting you try to coax an apology from your ex, however! Alexandra and Brian's situation will allow us to explain...

Alexandra and Brian's six-year marriage felt suffocating to Alex. Brian controlled every aspect of their lives — from deciding what meals she'd cook to what vacations they'd take as a family. When she wanted to go back to school and get a college degree, Brian decided that that would place too much stress on the family and it would be a waste of time for Alex.

Feeling unhappy and as if she was living the life only Brian wanted her to live, Alexandra filed for a divorce. Brian, however, just did not understand what she was unhappy about. "I take care of you and the kids," Brian told her. "There's nothing you want that I don't buy for you. I don't see why you feel unhappy."

Following the divorce, Brian still tried to make decisions for her. When she felt he was controlling her, she got angry, and a fight ensued. Because she often felt he was trying to tell her what to do, there were frequent conflicts. Disliking conflict, Alexandra tried to cut off all contact with him. However, she couldn't really do that as they shared in raising two children. Their frequent battles continued, and Alex told Brian they were his fault and caused by his attempts to run her life. Brian said that if Alex only understood how much he still loved her and wanted the best for her, she and he would get along well.

Alexandra's therapist suggested that she apologize to Brian to see if that could improve their relationship and their ability to co-parent. "But that would confirm to him that he was right and I was wrong," Alexandra protested. "That will just make him worse."

The therapist persisted, noting that things could not get much worse and it was worth a try. Alexandra finally gave in and agreed to apologize to Brian. She arranged to meet him at her therapist's office with her therapist present. Brian readily agreed to meet her. During the session, Alexandra said to Brian, "I asked you here to apologize to you for everything I've done to hurt you. I know that you love our children as much as I do and that you loved me too. I always saw you as controlling and trying to run my life. I know that you didn't intentionally try to make me unhappy. I apologize for the divorce and for the fights and arguments we've had since the divorce. Will you forgive me?"

Brian didn't know what to say at first and he looked at the therapist, who indicated he could reply to Alexandra. "Of course, I forgive you. I still love you and I wish we could start over."

"That can't happen," Alexandra said. "However, I am sincerely sorry for the ways I've hurt you."

"Couldn't we try it again?" Brian asked.

"No," she replied, "but I think we could be friends. As long as you accept me as a person who is equal to you and who can make her own decisions, I can be your friend."

"I think I can do that," Brian said. "I know you see me as trying to control you. And maybe I do that a little..."

"How about a lot?" the therapist interjected.

"Okay," Brian said sheepishly, "you've got me there. I will try to let her be her own person, though. I always thought I was doing that, but I guess I wasn't very good at it."

"No, you weren't," Alexandra said. "But I wasn't good at letting you know how I felt, either."

Alexandra and Brian parted this session as better friends and, they hoped, better co-parents. All it took was Alexandra's courage to offer an apology for something she once felt she didn't owe.

What an Apology Does

The founders of Alcoholics Anonymous figured out a long time ago that there is value in a well-spoken and sincere apology. In the twelve-step program of guiding principles outlining a course of action for recovery from alcoholism, two of the twelve steps involve examining past errors with the help of a sponsor (experienced member) and making amends for those errors. The last part means that an AA member, when he or she is ready to make amends, must apologize to those he or she has wronged (Steigerwald & Stone, 1999).

Apologies help because we all recognize that an apology is difficult. A sincere and genuine apology comes from the heart and says that you still care about the relationship; it acknowledges wrongdoing. When you apologize, you are admitting not only that you were wrong and you made a mistake but also that you recognize you are human and fallible. Whether you say that you are imperfect or not, the implication is there that what you did to hurt the other person was done not because you are perfect but because you were imperfect. This action of the imperfect man or woman — the apology — gives us the ability to forgive that person. You may not be willing to accept the apology of a person if you don't believe he thinks he was wrong, but it's different with an imperfect person. You can feel sorry for him — and forgiving. There's something healing about being apologized to by someone who is humbling himself before you.

How to Apologize Effectively to Your Co-Parent

- Pick a good time and place to apologize.
- Be sincere.
- Don't use an apology to try to "get back together" — simply use it to clear the air.
- Let it come from your heart.

A Good Apology

A good apology does come from the heart. And it is meant to acknowledge pain and hurt you have caused your co-parent. Of course, you should only use this strategy if you do, indeed, have something for which you need to apologize. Even if the pain and suffering you caused happened for a long time, an apology can be highly effective.

We all have much for which we could apologize. This is particularly true in a marriage that has ended. We suspect there is literally no end to the number of apologies both parties in a failed marriage could make. The good apology will focus on the past and on real actions that you know bothered or hurt your co-parent.

Eight Things for which You Could Apologize

- Filing for a divorce
- Not accepting your ex's imperfections
- Having an affair
- Being too controlling
- Keeping secrets
- Working too much
- Using alcohol or drugs
- Saying negative things about your co-parent to the children

It is amazing how powerful this one step can be in moving away from an adversarial relationship and toward a working collaboration between you and your co-parent.

Quick Review

If your relationship with your co-parent is mired in conflict and vindictiveness, try an apology. An apology might be the last thing your co-parent expects to hear from you, but it might be so powerful that it upsets the balance and helps to move the relationship forward in a positive direction.

An apology can work if it is sincere, comes from the heart, and is for something you did to wrong your co-parent.

CHAPTER 7

The Courage to Forgive (or, Forgiving Your Co-Parent Frees You)

Does the idea of forgiving your co-parent sound repugnant to you? Does the thought of forgiving her feel like you'd have to forget how she hurt you? Would forgiveness suggest that you would be condoning her reprehensible behavior? Would forgiving her make you feel weak?

Here's how *Merriam-Webster's Third New International Unabridged Dictionary* defines the word "forgive":

> 1 : to cease to feel resentment against on account of wrong committed : give up claim to requital from or retribution upon (an offender) : ABSOLVE, PARDON. 2 a : to give up resentment of or claim to requital for (an offense or wrong) : remit the penalty of. b : to grant relief from : refrain from exacting.

This definition says nothing about forgetting about or condoning an offense, nor does it say anything about the forgiving person appearing weak. It simply says that by forgiving you give up your resentment and your anger as well as your desire to punish.

When you hold on to your anger and resentment, you suffer. In fact, researchers have found that hostility is related to a range of physical problems, including increased blood pressure and heart problems (Iribarren et al., 2000; Niaura et al., 2002). There are additional ways that holding on to your hostility, anger, and resentment can hurt you. By focusing on your negative feelings, you are less able to concentrate on your responsibilities as a parent. Furthermore, when you think too much about your anger, you are giving away your power as an individual while at the same time diminishing your ability to focus on the purpose and the meaning of your life.

Bishop Desmond Tutu once said that there's nothing more destructive than resentment, anger, and revenge. "In a way," Bishop Tutu said, "to forgive is the best form of self-interest, because I'm also releasing myself from the bonds that hold me captive, and it's important that I do all I can to restore [the] relationship. Because without a relationship, I am nothing, I will shrivel" (Lipman, 2010).

A great South African political leader who knew about suffering and the potential corrosive effects of anger and resentment, Bishop Tutu perhaps has it right when he says there is nothing more destructive than anger and resentment. When we can't let these negative feelings go, we are bound with that other person in an unhealthy relationship that can destroy us.

So why is it so difficult for us to forgive, particularly when we realize that our anger and resentment are slowly killing us, or at least robbing us of the enjoyment of life? Maybe it's because it means we would have to give up our anger. Maybe it's because we believe that giving up those negative emotions toward our co-parent would make us vulnerable to being hurt again. Or, maybe it's because we feel it would weaken us in some essential way.

Forgiving is not an easy thing to do. When we've been holding on to our anger and resentment for a long time, forgiving requires courage and strength. Gandhi said as much when he said this: "The weak can never forgive. Forgiveness is the attribute of the strong" (Gandhi quotations, 1994-2007).

You Can Be Strong by Forgiving Your Co-Parent

We said in chapter 6 that a sincere apology can move your relationship forward. Now, we are advocating forgiveness. An apology is different from forgiveness. You have to acknowledge that you wronged your co-parent when you apologize. In order to forgive, you have to accept that he or she wronged you. But, at the same time, you are sending a very clear message that you are strong enough and have enough compassion to forgive, even if you never receive an apology in return.

Holding on to Your Anger and Resentment Can Kill You

Edward Hallowell, in his book *Dare to Forgive* (Hallowell, 2004), points out that recent research has given us important information about the unhealthy aspects of holding on to anger as well as about the freedom that forgiveness brings about.

Anger is a normal, healthy emotion and just like any other feeling you have. However, anger involves not only a psychological component (how you feel at the moment) but also a physiological component. The physiological aspect of anger relates to how your body responds to this emotion. Physical reactions usually involve muscle tension, an increase in heart rate, and elevation of your blood pressure as your body releases adrenaline.

What Happens When You Are Feeling Angry?

When you get angry, your body chemistry changes. Your blood pressure increases, and your immune system is suddenly activated. Your body tenses, and your stress levels are greatly heightened. If you are frequently angry with your co-parent over any extended period of time, these physiological reactions keep happening over and over again.

However, your body was not designed to endure continual anger. It's not that anger is an inherently "bad" emotion. In fact, there are very useful aspects of anger; it can help you identify a problem in your life that requires some action, for instance. But anger can be a destructive emotion if you keep it around too long.

The Destructive Aspects of Anger for Lynne

After almost ten years of marriage, Lynne filed for a divorce because, as she explained it to her husband Dennis, "I'm tired of living alone." Lynne had gradually become more angry and resentful over the years because his job seemed to demand that he spend long hours away from home. Lynne eventually concluded that he enjoyed being at meetings, traveling, and going out for business lunches and dinners. He apparently loved working more than he loved her or the children.

After the divorce, every time that Dennis was late picking up the kids, Lynne's mind flashed back to the countless dinners she had eaten alone because he had to work late. On the occasions when he didn't show up at all for his parenting time, she was reminded of her previous feelings of abandonment and rage that she experienced when he didn't come home. "When we were married," Lynne recalled, "I always felt that the children and I were not important enough for him to come home to." And when he missed the children's Little League games, school conferences, and Brownie meetings, she would go over in her mind the many ways he had let them down over the years.

Although Dennis seemed to be highly stressed almost all the time, it was Lynne who suffered from the physiological aspects of her anger at Dennis for never doing what he promised he would do. When he was late picking up the children, it was just as if he was doing it to her. During the final year of their marriage, as her anger grew stronger and more intense, Lynne began to suffer physical symptoms. She gained weight, her blood pressure increased, and she was experiencing panic attacks. Her internist said he could find no physical reason and he recommended that she see a therapist.

In therapy, Lynne began to realize that her intense anger toward Dennis was making her ill, and if she wanted to avoid serious health problems, she had to get out of the marriage. Although getting a divorce helped, Lynne realized that just getting a divorce didn't take all her anger away. For one thing, Dennis's behavior still affected her. "I would make plans on his weekends with the kids," Lynne said, "but he'd always call at the last minute and say he couldn't take the kids because something came up at work. That made me furious!"

For another thing, she also had to deal with the children's disappointment at having been repeatedly let down by their father. "I was an adult and it made me angry," Lynne said. "But the children just couldn't understand why he wouldn't do what he promised he would do. I usually ended up feeling like I had to defend him when I wanted to tell the children that if he really loved them he would keep his promises."

Lynne never thought about forgiving Dennis. Instead, she focused on her anger and how he was ruining her life and their children's lives. She reasoned that she was justified in her anger. "After all," she told a friend, "he would make anybody furious. I have every right to be bitter, vengeful, and very, very angry."

When her therapist suggested she forgive Dennis, Lynne felt irritated and betrayed. "Forgive him!" she snapped. "He doesn't deserve my forgiveness. He should lose all rights to his kids!"

"It's not for him," her therapist replied gently. "It's for you."

"I can't forgive him," was all Lynne could manage as a response.

Like many angry co-parents, Lynne found forgiveness to be a difficult remedy to apply. Edward Hallowell has said that it's so hard we'd sometimes rather die than try, especially when the hurt runs deep and has run so for a long time. If you're like Lynne, you might feel the same way: that forgiving your co-parent is impossible. Forgiveness may feel impossible because you believe that your marriage or a great part of your life has been ruined by what your co-parent has done.

Forgiveness as a Remedy for Anger

No matter how angry and resentful you may feel, however, keep your mind open to the options you have. Forgiveness is one of those options. No matter what your co-parent has done to you or your children, you can still forgive this person who has wronged you. If you can forgive him or her, you're the one who benefits the most.

How will you benefit?

When you forgive, you free yourself from your self-imposed prison cell of anger. Not only do you gain release from your anger and other negative feelings, but there will be physical benefits as well.

As both Hallowell and Frederick Luskin, Ph.D., who has headed the Stanford Forgiveness Project at Stanford University, have pointed out, there are several health benefits of forgiveness. Among those health benefits are these:

- Your blood pressure may go down.
- Your resting heart rate may decrease.
- Your immune system may get stronger.
- Your susceptibility to a heart attack or a stroke may decrease.
- You may decrease the number of physical symptoms you have, including headaches, backaches, and neck pain (Luskin, 2003).

Then, too, there are the emotional benefits. Forgiving can lift your spirits. It makes you feel happier, and it clarifies your thinking. No longer must you carry around the awful burden of your anger and resentment. Compared to other measures people take to improve their life, says Hallowell, forgiving is at least as good for you as losing weight, getting the right amount of sleep, taking supplemental vitamins, or wearing seat belts (Hallowell, 2004). Although, as we stated above, forgiving is hard to learn to do, you *can* do it.

How Do You Go about Forgiving Your Co-Parent?

Everett Worthington, Ph.D. at Virginia Commonwealth University, has developed and researched a model of forgiveness that is based on five steps:

1. Recalling the hurt
2. Developing empathy for the one who hurt you
3. Being grateful for the forgiveness you have received in your life
4. Committing to forgiveness
5. Holding on to forgiveness (Worthington, 2001)

Once you have decided to forgive your co-parent, Worthington's five steps are important in order to take the necessary action to forgive. We recommend the following practical steps to accomplish forgiveness:

Step 1. Write down in a notebook or journal all the ways your co-parent has hurt you. Write down everything that comes to mind. And continue writing until you have written down every injustice you can think of.

Step 2. In your notebook or journal, record all the ways your anger and resentment are hurting you. Is it keeping you from moving on in new relationships? Does it consume your thinking so that you are unproductive at work or at home? Are your friends tired of your constant anger? Are you saying things to your children that hurt them or undermine their feelings toward their other parent? Are you experiencing physical symptoms that may be related to your intense anger?

Step 3. Write down what you and your children will gain from you forgiving your co-parent. Spend some quiet time visualizing what you and your life would be like if you no longer felt so much anger and resentment. What would an anger-free life be like for you? Imagine the look on your children's faces if you could speak about their other parent without anger, cynicism, or sarcasm. Picture yourself talking to friends without ranting about your ex. Keep at this step until you can visualize yourself as a person who has let go of your anger and resentment in all of your important situations and relationships.

Step 4. Make the commitment to forgive him or her. (If you're not ready for step 4, go back and work more on steps 1 through 3.) If you are ready to make this commitment, tell the people closest to you that you are forgiving your co-parent. The more people you tell, the easier it will be to do. But keep in mind that some of the people in your life may not be ready themselves to forgive your co-parent or to let you forgive. You may have to avoid them — or win them over to your position.

Step 5. Replace your old, angry thoughts with newer ones that show empathy for your co-parent. For example, if you used to think, "She's trying to turn the children against me," try to find a new thought that will be more empathic, such as, "She felt so insecure; she thought if the children loved me, they couldn't also love her." Or, if your old thought was, "He loved work more than he loved me," your new thought could be, "He grew up thinking that he would be a good husband and a good father if he worked hard and made a comfortable living."

These are the important preliminary steps in forgiveness. As you practice these five steps, be aware that resentment and anger are habits, just like other bad habits. If you want to change your habits of feeling resentment and anger toward your co-parent, it will take about twenty-five days. That's the time it takes to bring about a change in most of our habits. Thus, in order to stop feeling all the negative things you feel toward your co-parent, you need to do this exercise each time you think of your co-parent for at least the next twenty-five days. But once you've begun to change your habits, you will also find that they no longer have the power to make you feel angry because you will have reprogrammed your own reactions. And when this happens, you start to become free.

There Is Still a Final Step in Forgiving Your Co-Parent

If you've accomplished the first five steps, you've made tremendous progress. You know you need to forgive your co-parent, and you recognize the benefits that will result from your forgiveness. Keep in mind before you go further that we're not suggesting that you get back together with your co-parent or that you become the best of friends. We are recommending that you forgive him or her in order to resolve your conflicts with each other, clear the air a bit, improve the understanding and communication between the two of you, and improve your physical health. To take the final step, though, you have to reach way down inside and ask yourself something very important: *Am I willing to forgive my co-parent?* You might answer back that you enjoy your anger. Or that he or she doesn't deserve your forgiveness. Or that you're not ready. However, although you might not be ready, you can bet your children are. For the children involved in postdivorce conflict, you must learn to forgive. For the sake of the children you love with all your heart, you must take the final, excruciatingly painful step and model the most magnanimous and humbling of all acts — the act of forgiveness.

Step 6. Perform the forgiveness exercise. If you think you are ready to take this step, here's how you can do it.

☐ In your notebook or journal write out your forgiveness statement:

I _____ do hereby grant forgiveness to _____.

I forgive you for _____

_____

_____

Here's what I need to say to you so that my offering of forgiveness will be complete:

_____

_____

_____.

☐ Having filled out this forgiveness statement, put it up somewhere in your house (perhaps on the front of your refrigerator) so you can read it every day for a few days.

☐ In thinking about forgiving your co-parent, it may or may not be important to express this to her or him directly. We believe it generally is very valuable to offer your forgiveness statement aloud and in person. The next part of this last step, therefore, is to arrange a time and place to deliver your verbal forgiveness.

☐ The final step is to meet with your co-parent and give your forgiveness statement aloud.

Here is the way Bakari forgave Andrea:

"I, Bakari, grant forgiveness to my co-parent Andrea. I forgive you for divorcing me and for telling the children I have not been a good father. The reason I am forgiving you is because I can no longer walk around with anger in my heart toward you."

And, this is the way Evette forgave Steven:

"I, Evette, forgive you, Steven. I forgive you for being abusive to me and for threatening me. I also forgive you for trying to take away physical custody of the children from me. The reason I am forgiving you is because I have come to be at peace with who you are and I want to be the kind of person that my children can learn the art of forgiveness from."

Remember What Forgiveness Is Not

One of the biggest challenges to forgiveness is the belief that forgiving the offense, such as an affair, means that you condone it. This is not true. Forgiveness does not mean that you have concluded that his or her behavior was acceptable or justified. Nor does it mean that you will reconcile with the person who has wronged you. It only means that you are changing how you personally will deal with the wrongs done to you and how you will deal with your anger.

Quick Review

If you don't forgive someone who has wronged you, you run the risk of holding on to anger and resentment. If you hold on to anger and resentment, you can make your own life miserable. A vindictive, angry mind-set creates bitterness, increases stress levels, and can diminish overall health.

The steps to forgiveness include recognizing the reasons for your anger, listing the benefits of letting go of your resentment and anger, and committing yourself to forgiving your co-parent. Follow the practical steps in this chapter to recall your hurts, commit yourself to forgiving, and then hold on to the forgiveness. The final step may be to deliver a forgiveness statement in person — and aloud — to your co-parent.

Understanding and Using Your Power Effectively

Dana always feels like she comes out on the wrong end of any conflict with Gary, her former husband.

"He can be so slick," she complains. "After all, he's a trial lawyer and he's very good at his job. He knows how to win people over, and his goal is always to come out on top."

Dana says she can't bring anything to his attention about their children because he will twist it around and convince her and anyone else he talks to that it was her problem and something she caused. During the divorce, Gary knew the judge handling their case and he knew the court system inside and out. She felt she got taken to the cleaners financially in the divorce, and she still resents this.

When asked, Gary presents himself as the victim of an unstable ex-wife. He says that her mental health problems interfere with her ability to take care of the children, and he cites numerous examples of her acting in obstinate ways that clearly were not in the best interests of the children.

"Gary knew how to play the system and I was like a babe in the woods," Dana says. "Even if I could have afforded a more high-powered attorney, I think he still would have won."

Over the nearly two years since their divorce, Dana has felt more powerless and more depressed. Dana says and does things out of anger that prompt the court to back Gary even more, and her actions seem to support his presentation of her as unstable. Most recently, Dana refused to take the children to a weekend soccer game in which the kids were involved. Gary had signed the kids up, and most of the time Dana was cooperative. However, by not taking the kids to their game, she again set the scene for Gary to file a motion for violation of the court order. It's likely the court will once again decide in Gary's favor.

Who Has the Power?

The word *power* conjures up a variety of unpleasant and socially unpopular images and reactions. People aren't supposed to think in terms of power, right?

The fact is, though, you and everyone else deal with power every day in every interaction. Power is not just what abusive people manipulate. Power is also the impulse that leads you to dress a certain way, drive the car you do, and decide who you will speak to first at the meeting or barbeque. Each decision and each choice of words are part of an attempt to wield as much influence, or power, as you can.

As you interact with people, a silent voice is listing the reasons for your choices. The voice is saying,

- I want them to like me.
- I want to look intelligent, not stupid.
- I want them to think my child is as good as theirs.
- I want them to agree with me.
- I want them to think I make sense.
- I want them to agree to do what I'm asking them to do.

This is a partial list of the many issues that make power important in relationships. In divorce, it's even more important because you're trying to keep some semblance of control over your life and the lives of your children.

As you divorce and even afterward, the justice system may also make power a critical issue as you struggle to secure a good attorney and obtain a legal outcome favorable to you. One radio commercial for a group of divorce lawyers for men says, "You don't have to lose your house, your retirement account, your money, or your children." If it was true that you didn't have to lose any of these things, then they seem to be saying that they plan to help you take everything and not leave anything for your former wife. They're also saying, "We're really powerful and we can make sure things turn out just the way you want them to." Most importantly, they're saying that if you choose the right lawyer, you'll have more power.

The traditional way of looking at power in divorce is in the form of a question. That question is "Who will win and who will lose?" However, considering that the power is coming from lawyers and courts, a lawyer may be offering you a false sense of power. In other words, you may not really have any control over what happens.

The loss of control that people feel during a divorce makes them willing to spend significant amounts of money on the promise of power. In the court process, power is given to you or you buy it. But you aren't being taught how to understand the natural power balance that exists between two people in a marriage — or a divorce. That's what we help you with in this chapter. We'll teach you how to understand and use the natural power balance to improve your life, your co-parent's life, and especially your children's lives.

Understanding How Power Works

We will show you how to assess the power balance in your divorce. Once you understand this, you can move on to rebalancing the power in a healthy way. There are two concepts that you must grasp to work with power and create change in your divorce situation.

Power Concept One

The person who has less power in a relationship will develop symptoms. Below is a partial list of the symptoms that a disempowered parent may develop. Try to look at this exercise with an unemotional eye. Don't judge the meaning of these symptoms until later in the chapter. We're suggesting that power imbalance is one of the most common

---

**Common Symptoms of Divorced Co-Parents
Suffering a Loss of Power**

- Depression/Anxiety
- Aggression
- Jealousy
- Substance abuse
- New symptoms of mental illness
- Openly violating court orders
- Compulsive phone calls, emails, text messages, etc.
- Loss of boundaries with the children (becoming so entangled with one's children's feelings that you can't separate emotionally from your children)

reasons for a person to develop these kinds of symptoms, but keep in mind that there can be other reasons. These symptoms may describe you, or they may describe your co-parent.

Power Concept Two

If you are experiencing less power than your co-parent, you may recognize some of these symptoms. You may well refuse to let anyone else change you or improve your situation. When you see that you are causing problems in your relationship with your co-parent and that you are unwilling to let anyone help, you have been given a clear signal that power is the central issue. After all, if you refuse to let others help you or change you, you have control over something important; you have a troubled form of power that you unwittingly developed.

If you have genuine, healthy power and you develop any of the above symptoms, you are more likely to ask for and accept help to recover in a reasonable length of time. When you are too greatly troubled or upset by your loss of power, you will resist anyone's efforts to help you.

What Is the Power Balance in Your Divorce?

You can figure out the power balance in your divorce by using the following scale. On a scale of 1 to 10, put a number beside each of the nine factors below. Out of the 10 points that each will be worth, what percentage of the power in each area do you have and what percentage does your former spouse have? The two numbers on each line should add up to 10. For instance, if you feel your co-parent is better off financially, you may assess that he has seven points (70 percent) of the power and you have three points (30 percent) of the total power. Put only a number from 1 to 10 on each line.

If there is a significant difference between the points that each of you has after you have made an objective assessment in this scale, the one with the lower score may be suffering from disempowerment. This will help explain you or your co-parent's symptoms and is likely to also help explain some of the bad behavior either you or your co-parent displays.

Assessing the Power Balance in Your Divorce Scale

1. Who is better off financially?   _____ _____

2. Who is more highly educated?   _____ _____

3. Who came out better in the divorce in general?   _____ _____

4. Who wanted the divorce?   _____ _____

5. Who do the children prefer or side with?   _____ _____

6. Who is the more sympathetic character in the eyes of friends and relatives?   _____ _____

7. Who actively practices his or her religion and takes the children to religious services?   _____ _____

8. Who has more time with the children?   _____ _____

9. Who knows more about the children's lives?   _____ _____

Total Points Each: _____ _____

For instance, in the example at the beginning of this chapter, Dana made a strong case for her being the disempowered parent. However, she isn't connecting her depression or angry and immature actions to the power imbalance. She feels like a victim and believes she's helpless to change anything. If she understands that her symptoms are being caused by the power imbalance, she can take steps to get control of her life back and focus on the areas where her power is poor compared to Gary's.

If you have the lower score and are suffering, look at each of the items of power listed above and see which ones you can make changes in to reclaim your power. Could you explore spirituality with the children? Would a decision to act charitably toward friends and relatives on either or both sides increase your power? Do you need to lighten up in your discipline with the kids? For instance, if you're trying to be a heavy-duty disciplinarian, you may want to lighten up and have more fun with them.

Likewise, if your co-parent is the one with the symptoms, look at what you can do to help put some power back into his or her hands. Do something that you wouldn't ordinarily do. For example, if there is a field trip at school that you would normally go on, offer it to your co-parent first. If you are the mother and there's a father-daughter dance coming up, see what you can do to facilitate making it happen for your daughter. If your co-parent is having trouble making ends meet, buy some extra clothes for the kids to send to your co-parent's house. Ask and consider your co-parent's opinion about something in your child's life. Do you often find yourself giving your co-parent a list of things to do or not do with the children? Try stepping back and letting him or her figure it out. If you're the one getting the list, try taking back your power by thanking your co-parent for the input (but not in a snarky way!).

Okay, we can hear you saying, "But I already do too much." This may be true. Therefore, you have to coordinate your changes with the items that show the greatest imbalance. For instance, if the children are negative toward your co-parent, make sure you encourage them to speak well of her or him. Say some kind and favorable things about your co-parent to them. No, you're not lying by speaking well of your co-parent even when you consider him or her quite lame. What you as an adult know or feel to be true and what you should share with your kids can be two different things. You thought carefully about what you said during the marriage, and it's just as important to think carefully about what you say during and after your divorce.

Is there something that you know your co-parent wants and you've been unwilling to concede it because of your anger? Is it something that you really won't miss? If in the scale above you answered that you came out generally better than your co-parent, this would be a good area in which to make concessions.

Whatever changes you make, you'll need to work at those areas of power imbalance for a month or more before expecting to notice significant changes. Your hard work and sacrifice will pay off. Some changes may happen quickly, but don't get discouraged if you have to watch for a while before getting the payoff.

Quick Review

When there is an imbalance of power in the relationship you have with your co-parent, you or your co-parent may suffer some of the symptoms listed in this chapter. Fill out the brief questionnaire to better understand the nature of the balance or imbalance of power between you and your co-parent. To reduce the conflict or the symptoms either of you may experience, work at balancing the power. When the power is balanced, you, your co-parent, and your children will benefit.

CHAPTER 9

Picturing Your Children: Why Do You Need a Relationship with Your Co-Parent?

The fact is you don't need to maintain a relationship with the person you were once married to or the person you once lived with — unless, that is, you have a child whom you and your co-parent will raise together. Then you need to have a relationship that allows you to co-parent together.

If you're going to co-parent effectively, you need to have a relationship that is cordial enough that you can do all those things that co-parents do together.

> Leslie found this out after she got divorced. She admits that she somehow thought that after divorcing Richard life would be easier and she wouldn't have to deal with him. "That's not at all the way it was," Leslie says. "We both wanted to be there on the day Zoë started kindergarten. We both wanted to go to the pediatrician appointments with her. And when there was the first school conference with her teacher, we were both there. Sometimes I felt like I saw more of him after the divorce than before the divorce."

> Ryan felt something similar. "I determined that I wasn't going to be one of those fathers who never spent time with his kids," he said. "I wanted to be a part of their lives. I wanted to talk to them every day. I wanted to be with them on their birthdays and I wanted to attend every baseball game, every soccer game, every Cub Scout meeting, and every dance recital. That meant that Letta and I had to be together a lot as well."

> And Sarah, too, found that her co-parent became a big part of her life. "When we'd go to our son's basketball games, he'd always say to the first parent who arrived, 'Make sure you save a seat for Dad (or Mom).' So he sort of forced us to sit together. We both knew that he'd look to see if we were sitting together."

It's about the Kids

The relationship between you and your co-parent is not about you. It's about the children. It's about what it feels like as a child if your parents are always fighting and in conflict. Children often see themselves as the reason for the fighting between their parents. Therefore, it is very stressful for kids when their parents fight. They are likely to blame themselves, and they are likely to be just as anxious and unhappy as their parents are (Grych, Harold, & Miles, 2003).

In order for you to create a secure and predictable environment for your child, you have to make sure there is little conflict and little or no fighting in that environment. This means that you have to understand that the best reason to get along with your co-parent is to give your child an excellent opportunity to grow up secure, confident, and well adjusted. To do that, you must remember that you're not trying to get along with your co-parent to reconcile, live together again, or be the best of friends. You're doing it to make life more enjoyable for your child. Is there any better reason?

> Hannah and Randy hadn't even noticed how far apart they had grown emotionally until Hannah had an affair with the neighbor. It was a short affair, but when Randy found out he was devastated. After much soul searching Hannah told Randy that she wanted a divorce. She had changed and was no longer happy in their marriage even though Randy was a good guy. Despite his hurt, Randy continued to treat Hannah respectfully, and they were able to work out custody issues and parenting time before they went to court.
>
> After the divorce, they didn't talk much but were able to work things out with a minimum of conflict. Their three young boys rarely saw them argue and never heard a negative word about the other parent. The children always got what they needed (medically and emotionally) because their parents continued to put their needs first. Hannah and Randy did not do everything the same but did allow the other to parent his or her own way. Randy probably let the kids stay up later than Hannah did, and Hannah might have been a little rigid, but the kids knew what to expect from each parent and knew that they could not get their parents to fight over little things.

Divorce can be a lesson that teaches children how to solve disputes in a mature and reasonable way despite the pain and loss, like Randy and Hannah's family, or it can be like Jenna's family.

Jenna's parents divorced when she was just six, but they fought her entire life. They argued and screamed when they were married, and they continued to fight after the divorce until Jenna left home to go to college. Jenna avoided going home because of the stress of the fighting and the stress of "choosing" with whom she would stay. She had lots of boyfriends at college, but relationships did not last for her, and she blamed her parents for that. She too was critical and judgmental in her relationships, and that made a lasting relationship difficult. When Jenna realized this, she also realized how much her parents had influenced her.

Your children are watching you deal with one another. They watch while you stand on the porch and wave bills at each other or roll your eyes and criticize each other for the infraction of the moment. They see the hand gestures you make as you drive away. They are listening while you yell at each other on the phone even though you think they're asleep. They know you want to ruin each other financially and emotionally because of the affair or the abuse or other adult transgressions that they do not fully understand except that they must be very bad. They see their parents consumed by resentment, anger, and a desire for revenge against people they love.

Is this what you want for your children? Of course not! Nobody wants to teach his or her children to be vindictive and spiteful. You want your children to be caring, reasonable, and forgiving people. It doesn't matter if you preach these values to your children or take them to church — they are learning from your behaviors.

So how do you teach children (and yourself) to cope with a significant loss? And how do you successfully deal with the uncertainty and changes that come with such an enormous life change as divorce? Think about your children and what they need from you. Think about how you want them to treat people during a conflict. Consider how you want them to communicate with others even if they are angry. How do you teach them to see the value in empathizing with others even when they do not agree?

Picture Your Child

In some of our groups for co-parents in high-conflict relationships, we ask co-parents to bring photos of their children to the group.

Then, while showing other group members the photos of the kids, we want them to talk about their children. This always results in parents talking proudly about their kids, telling about how they're doing in school, their personalities at home, and their successes in extracurricular activities. Most parents have a special beam on their faces when they're talking about their children. For most of us, our children are what make life exciting and pleasant.

After parents have had the opportunity to share their descriptions of their children and do a little boasting about them, we tell parents to remember that that's why they are in the group: to make life better for their children.

Sure, they need to resolve conflicts with their co-parent. And, yes, they need to be able to exchange information, communicate about the next football practice, and talk about the medication that's been prescribed for their child. But more than anything, it's about being civil to one another so their child grows up in an atmosphere that says, "We love you enough to get along with each other even though we can't live with each other."

> When you are having difficulty controlling your anger or finding common ground with your co-parent, keep one picture in your mind: the face of your child.

What Kind of Model Do You Want to Be for Your Kids?

What do you want to teach your children? What do you want to model for your children? Do you want your children to learn:

- To be unreasonably angry?
- To seek revenge against those who have done them wrong?
- To let their hostility and resentment turn into a vendetta against another person?
- To be a failure at resolving conflicts?
- To hold on to their anger and bitterness?
- To let unresolved feelings become self-destructive habits?

If you do, just maintain your anger, hostility, and resentment toward your co-parent. Your children will readily learn these things from you. But if you want just the opposite for your children, you must make sure you model the kinds of behavior and actions you want them to exhibit in their life.

It's very simple. Your children are learning from you every minute of every day. They watch you to see how you handle your feelings, how you resolve conflicts, how you deal with your anger, and how you treat their other parent. They will soak all this up, and if your actions are not a model of civility, restraint, and propriety, they will learn that this is the way they should handle situations that arise in their life.

Children Learn from Watching Their Parents Interact with One Another

How do you and your co-parent interact with each other? Do you swear at each other? Do disagreements always end in raised voices and tears? Do you show disrespect to each other? Do your children see you and your co-parent being unfriendly, gruff, surly, or hateful to each other?

These questions are important for you as you plan how you will help your child shape his ideas about what relationships should be like. Model for your child the type of relationship that you would like him to be involved in one day. Don't feel like he should never see his parents disagree or that you can't ever express displeasure with your co-parent in his presence. However, do remember that your child is watching and your relationship may be the standard that he uses to follow in his own relationships in the future. Are you and your co-parent the example you want him to follow?

What Does Your Child Come to See as Most Important to You?

You may think that you are just trying to express your displeasure or anger with your co-parent. You might even rationalize that seeing you and your co-parent stand up to each other or disagree about an issue is important so your child learns she doesn't always have to give in to others. However, she may also be learning something quite different than you think when she's watching and listening to your interactions with your co-parent.

For instance, she may actually be learning that you don't care as much about her as you do about fighting with your co-parent. Or she might be learning that you are angry too often about little and inconsequential matters. Or that not communicating is more important to you than communicating.

On the other hand, if your child sees you trying to communicate effectively with your co-parent, or if he sees you resolving issues without getting too angry, or if he sees you valuing a relationship with his other parent, he will learn that effective communication and his best interests are much more important to you than venting your anger or frustration.

What did you teach your child today?

You may be surprised to learn that it was much more than you realized. You have to remember that even if you have an infant, little eyes are always watching, and little ears are always listening, and children learn their most valuable lessons about life right at home by watching and listening to you.

> Don't worry that children never listen to you; worry that they are always watching you.
> — Robert Fulghum

Exercises to Help You Focus on What Is Important

Try these exercises to help you focus on what is important.

Exercise 1. Close your eyes and visualize your child grown up to age twenty-five. What kind of person has he become? What values and characteristics do you hope he exhibits?

Write down the qualities that are important to you. For instance, you may write down that honesty, integrity, and compassion are important values. Then, after you have made a list of the values you hold in high regard, next to each value write down how you are currently modeling these values for your child. If you are not doing as good a job as you think you should in teaching these values, write down how you might be undermining these values.

Finally, write down what you might do differently. Are there alternative ways you should be living? Should you be giving up the conflict with your co-parent? Or expressing it differently? Remember that remaining in conflict during your child's entire childhood is not likely to prepare her for successful long-term relationships.

Exercise 2. Imagine again that your child is grown up. And imagine her telling a boyfriend or significant other about her life growing up and how her parents handled the divorce. If things continue as they are, what will your child say about how you handled the divorce? What will she say about how it affected her? If you are able to become emotionally divorced and stop the ongoing turmoil, what do you hope your child will say about you? What do you want her to be able to say about how it affected her?

Quick Review

If you want to be a positive role model for your child, you must remember to act as you would have him act later on in life.

This is especially valuable if you have a highly conflicted relationship with your co-parent. Your children will learn about life and how to carry on relationships by watching you. If your relationship with your co-parent is marred by dissension, arguments, and anger, your children will learn that that's how relationships should be carried out.

To be a better role model, keep the face of your child always in your mind. You want the innocent face of your child to remind you that you must act toward your co-parent in a civil and respectful manner. Write down the lessons you hope to teach your children about how to get along with others, how to communicate, and how to resolve difficult issues as well as general values.

Write down the things that you already do that lend to this. What will you do differently?

Creating Your Own Healing Ritual

Think of the celebrations, the rites of passage, and the ceremonies commemorating milestone events we use in our society.

A first birthday party is a very special event that often features the whole family getting together along with friends and other children. There is a special birthday cake with one candle that the child is encouraged to try to blow out. This is followed by the child being allowed (often) to play with his slice of cake — usually making a complete mess of himself and everyone close by. This is accompanied by much hilarity, photos, videos, and gifts.

Graduation from high school means weeks of preparation. On the day of graduation, in front of an audience of hundreds of friends and relatives, the graduates, clad in elaborate caps and gowns, parade into an auditorium. There are speeches, music, and finally the ritual handing out of diplomas. Then, following the graduation ceremony, the graduates make their round of parties where they are greeted by well-wishers, and there is much talk about the future and the significance of this milestone event.

And the most memorable ceremony of all — your wedding. Planned for months, if not years, a wedding may be a very expensive celebration. Marriage rituals include engagement parties, showers, bachelor and bachelorette parties, the choice of dresses, tuxedos, flowers, and a cake and a carefully selected invitation that is sent to hundreds of your closest friends and relatives. The ceremony often takes place in a religious institution, where sacred vows are proclaimed and the religious leader sanctifies the union of the two people. Later there is a reception that involves a feast, music, dancing, toasts, and speeches. But the celebration doesn't end after the reception. There may be a honeymoon, which gives the couple a chance to adjust to each other in a relaxed setting.

What do these rituals and ceremonies do for you? They mark the passage of time; they signify a milestone event; they help ease and publicize an important transition; they celebrate an ending or a beginning; they are a public statement or an acknowledgement of a transition from one stage of life to another. For most of these ceremonies and celebrations — along with others such as quinceañeras, sweet sixteen parties, baptisms, confirmations, bat and bar mitzvahs, anniversary parties, and funerals — we are surrounded by family and friends, usually all the people we love and care about the most.

But what happened when you got a divorce?

The chances are that you showed up on a certain day and waited in the hallway or an unfriendly courtroom for your name to be called. Accompanied by your attorney, you were asked a few brief, perfunctory questions and you answered in a similar perfunctory manner. The judge declared that you were officially divorced and signed the judgment of divorce. You then left the courtroom alone (unless you brought a friend for moral support) and walked out into a hallway filled with people going about their own busy lives. And you were expected to adjust and get over it very quickly and get on with your life.

But a divorce is as important as other milestones in life; some might argue that it's even more significant than some events that are typically marked by a ritual. The reason is that a divorce involves significant loss. If someone close to you dies, you lose one person. If you divorce, you lose not only one person — someone whom you once loved — but possibly also your entire family and the people who provided you the most significant support system you had. As a result, there should be a grieving period. And the loss should be given its due through a ceremony, a ritual, a rite of passage. But it's not.

You could go to a divorce support group. But a support group doesn't provide the same comfort as a stereotyped ritual. You are pretty much on your own to disentangle from the relationship with your partner. And there's no ritualized transition guiding you from married to single status. Indeed, although we expect couples with children to go from a troubled marriage to an amicable divorce, that transition is far from easy. And, again, society does little or nothing to support this major life transition. In short, divorce is distinguished by an absence of accepted rituals to acknowledge the enormous impact of this momentous, frequently turbulent shift in people's lives (Price, 1989).

Without guideposts for this journey, it is easy to get stuck. The structure of a ceremony or a ritual helps you travel down an unfamiliar and uncertain path. Getting stuck on the path after divorce often means you haven't effectively severed your ties from your partner, and that may mean you are confronted with and at times overwhelmed by your fears, your sadness, and your anger. The biggest roadblock in this perilous journey you're on is holding on to your anger and resentment.

Furthermore, the sadness that accompanies divorce can feel as overwhelming as the grief that attends the death of a loved one. Because we're usually not taught how to handle this level of grief, we're uncomfortable with it; often newly divorced people try to cope with their grief by rewriting their entire marriage as a mistake from the beginning. People sometimes do this by reliving and remembering events in the marriage and reinterpreting those events to support their new belief that their spouse was always an awful person.

Holding on to the sadness and the anger deprives you of an opportunity to complete the grieving process. To fully grieve, you have to remember the good as well as the bad. You have to appreciate the closeness you once shared to experience the sadness you feel about the marriage going so wrong and to realize how mismatched you and your spouse were.

The stages of grieving the loss of a marriage are not so different from the stages outlined in the classic 1970 book *On Death and Dying*, written by Elizabeth Kubler-Ross. In her book, Kubler-Ross wrote that most people who experience a death will go through the stages denial, anger, bargaining, depression, and acceptance before coming to terms with their sadness. When you've experienced a difficult divorce, you may realize you've successfully come through the various stages when you have accepted the divorce and feel a level of peace in regard to it. No longer do you experience the passion and the emotional roller coaster rides that were once there.

Rituals Can Be Invaluable Tools

We have found rituals to be invaluable tools to help couples finally sever their emotional bonds — whatever the legal status of their relationship.

Sandra and Foster had been divorced for six years but were still as tangled up with each other as ever. Their only child was eight. Since their divorce, both had found all other relationships to be superficial. Yet, despite sincere attempts to get back together, the same struggles that ended their marriage tore them apart again and again. Like many couples, they couldn't be married and they couldn't let go of what their marriage might be. Their ability to ignore the reality of what their marriage had become held them together.

Initially, we tried to help them reconcile with each other. Then we asked if they would agree to an apparently crazy way of resolving their dilemma. They agreed; they no longer had anything to lose. They were given detailed directions to a small town in Michigan's upper peninsula and told to take along their old wedding rings.

With an air of dramatic expectancy, they set off on a fourteen-hour drive. Following instructions, they took a two-hour boat tour up the Lake Superior coastline, during which they spent the first part of the trip reviewing their life together. Once they were one hour out, they went to the upper deck of the boat. There, while holding hands, they cast their rings into one of the coldest, deepest lakes in the world, a lake whose reputation, we had reminded them, has always been to "never give up her dead."

With some couples, a divorce ritual like this leads to a renewed commitment and a decision to continue together in a new way. For others, it provides a way of bringing a difficult, ambivalent relationship to its conclusion. Foster and Sandra spoke little on their drive back. Upon their return, each later told us, they were filled with extreme sadness and then an understanding that it was time to let go. From this point they went their separate ways (Price, 1989).

But How Do You Go Your Separate Ways?

One way to get there is to remember. Remember as much as you can about your courtship and your marriage. Here are some ways to facilitate your memory of the events of your relationship with your former partner:

- Over a period of a few weeks, look through all the photos you can get your hands on. Haul out your wedding album, family photo albums, and all the pictures that tell the story of your life with your former spouse.

- Allow yourself to feel what you see in the photos. Remember all the events and circumstances surrounding each photo you find. What were you feeling then? Were they pleasant or unpleasant feelings?

- Stop if you begin to feel overwhelmed. But be sure to bring them out another time. Just don't shut off your feelings no matter how hard it is looking at the photos and even though remembering brings back a flood of emotions.

- On a set of note cards write down how you met, what you did on your first anniversary, the first gift you received as a couple, the first gifts you gave each other, and various other positive memories.

- On a different set of note cards (perhaps of a different color), write down the events and situations that made you feel hurt or pain. Take your time. This can also take weeks.

- With a photograph of your ex in front of you, read the cards aloud to her. Do this in private a number of times.

- Write a letter of thanks to your ex for all she gave you during the courtship and the marriage. Be open and honest, and look deep within yourself for the gratitude for all you feel she provided you. This can include feelings of love, a sense of protection or security, joy and enjoyment, or opportunities for you to grow. This may be a very difficult step, but if you were able to complete the previous steps you should now be open to the positive. This is a private letter that you will not share with anyone (unless you choose to do so).

Creating Your Emotional Divorce Ritual

A ritual is a very personalized way to respect and celebrate a major life event. It must be personalized and meaningful to you. You can probably design a much better ritual or ceremony for yourself than we could. However, here is an example of a ritual used by a co-parent we know.

Healing Ritual 1. Take the positive cards and tie them up with a ribbon, perhaps one from your wedding.

Healing Ritual 2. Choose a place where your ceremony will be held. It could be in your yard, a park, or a place where you and your ex share a common memory.

Healing Ritual 3. Use three special candles, one larger than the other two. Also, include flowers, matches, pictures from your wedding, and individual photos of each of you. You can choose to play music (the co-parent who created this ritual played songs that were popular during her marriage). Dress formally, as you would for a wedding or funeral. You also need a bowl in which to burn the cards with negative issues.

Healing Ritual 4. You may choose to invite close friends, family members, or even your ex. Or you can perform the ritual alone. And you may want to repeat it more than once.

Healing Ritual 5. On the appointed day, go to your ceremonial area and set up with the large candle between the two smaller candles. A wedding photo of the two of you should be placed behind the large candle; the individual photos of each of you should be placed behind one of the smaller candles.

Healing Ritual 6. Light the large candle, which symbolizes your marriage. Read aloud the thank you letter that you wrote to your ex.

Healing Ritual 7. Burn the negative cards in the bowl.

Healing Ritual 8. Take the large candle and light the smaller candles. As you do so, stand up the individual pictures.

Healing Ritual 9. Extinguish the large candle and gently turn the wedding photograph face down.

Healing Ritual 10. Close the ceremony with a statement about how it is now time to begin your lives anew as individuals who are both on new journeys. Wish your ex the best on his or her journey.

Healing Ritual 11. Have a moment of silence.

The Emotional Divorce Ritual Can Help You Move On

John and Kira had been divorced for five years, but they had continued fighting over almost every issue. John said he was sick of the fighting; however, he was at a loss as to what to do. He felt that it was all Kira's fault that they fought all the time. Yet, he felt trapped in a pattern of responding in the same old ways whenever they tried to communicate.

When his therapist told him that he was still emotionally married to Kira, John laughed derisively and said, "That's ridiculous. I hate her for what she's done to me over the past five years. The last thing I want is to be married to her — emotionally or any other way!"

When he came back the following week, however, he told his therapist that he had been thinking, and there might be a little truth to what she said. He revealed that his current wife certainly believed that he was emotionally connected to Kira, and his wife was fed up with the way they fought with each other.

John was told about a ritual for an emotional divorce and he agreed to work on it. He started by going through the photo album he still had. It was a small photo album, so he went to family members on both his side of the family and on Kira's side. He leafed through the albums numerous times before he was able to acknowledge any positives in his life with Kira.

When he got to the note cards, John was able to whip off thirty negatives in less than an hour. On the other hand, it took a month to write out the positive cards. He was ready to proceed with an emotional divorce ritual but got stuck when he found it all but impossible to write a thank you card to Kira. Initially, he just could not think of anything beyond "Thank you for our beautiful children."

After a few more weeks, he was able to allow himself to acknowledge debts of gratitude he owed Kira. He wrote that he was grateful for her loving him at a time in his life when he felt very insecure. John also thanked her for pushing him to apply for a better job — and helping him to get the job and become successful at it. Finally, he thanked her for the fun they had in the early part of the marriage when they enjoyed camping in state parks. John was now ready for his ceremony.

He chose to perform the ceremony in private. He didn't want anyone present — not even his current wife — because he didn't want to break down in front of anyone. But he went on alone with the ritual.

Afterward, he said he couldn't help crying and feeling a great deal of sadness. When it was over, he said he felt emotionally drained, but he also felt proud of himself because he did something that he believed was not only difficult but also very important to do. He concluded by saying, "I think I really am ready to move on with my life without Kira."

A Few Final Words about Other Divorce Rituals

It doesn't matter what kind of divorce ritual you create or use. There are numerous ritualized approaches you could use. For example, you could both melt down your wedding rings and forge them into new ones to symbolize your commitment to a fresh start. Or you and your co-parent could write out the details of your troubled past on note cards or collect artifacts and photos from your marriage and then dispose of them in a ritual fashion. Or why not a divorce modeled after a raucous New Orleans funeral? There would be mournful music played on the way to the ceremony and upbeat, high-stepping jazz afterward. Each spouse in turn, when asked whether he or she wished to continue to be married to the other, could respond, "I don't!" The minister could conclude the ceremony by saying, "I now pronounce you man and woman."

Quick Review

If you're stuck in a relationship with your co-parent in which there is considerable anger and conflict, consider that you may still be emotionally married. One way to achieve an emotional divorce is through an emotional divorce ritual. This involves looking at photographs of your courtship and wedding and of your life together after you got married. Then have a ceremony in which you relive the positive and negative emotions of the relationship and then bury the past, cut your emotional ties to your ex, and move on with your new life.

Strategies to Change
Your Co-Parent

CHAPTER 11

Relearning Basic Communication Techniques

You're a wonderful communicator. Everyone says so. At work you can communicate with the best of them. You can be assertive when you need to be. You know how to raise an issue with a colleague. You're great at letting everyone on your team know what's going on. People love you because you're sensitive, kind, and understanding.

So, why can't you communicate with your co-parent?

We know we shouldn't have asked...because we know exactly what you're going to say:

- "My communication skills are just fine; it's my ex who doesn't know how to communicate."
- "I gave up trying with her because she's so angry and vindictive. Who could use appropriate communication with a witch like her!"
- "He's been so angry and mean to me for so long, I don't care if I never talk to him again!"

It may not be your fault that you and your co-parent don't communicate. However, there is the possibility (however slight that possibility might be!) that you contribute to the messed-up communication between you. Therefore, in this chapter, we're going to review some basic communication techniques and remind you what you need to be doing in order to communicate better with the other parent of your children.

No matter what's going on between you and your co-parent, it's almost a certainty that communication has broken down and needs to be repaired. Not necessarily for you — although it may make life much more pleasant for both of you if communication is significantly improved — but for your kids. As one sixteen-year-old boy trying to get along with his divorced and constantly battling parents said recently, "I might as well be living in Iraq. It gets that bad sometimes being caught in the crossfire."

So what goes wrong in communication between co-parents caught in a sniping battle? It's usually one of these scenarios:

- One of you attacks the other. You always find out too late that there was a doctor's appointment, a school conference, or a soccer game. So you get out your cell phone, call her up, and say, "Thanks a lot for letting me know about Jennifer's dance recital! I'm a parent, too, you know. You have no right to not inform me about things going on in her life!"
- When you perceive you've being blamed or attacked, you get defensive. "I tried to call you, but you weren't answering my calls. Remember that! Besides that, if you ever took her to any of her dance rehearsals, you'd know what's going on!"
- Once attack, blame, and defensiveness occur, all bets are off — it's free-for-all time. "If I were more involved! Hah! You're a great one to talk! You're out whoring around with your new boyfriend; you could care less about our daughter! You just want to cut her out of my life. You think you're the only one who can parent her!"

Three Essential Communication Rules
1. Use "I" messages to initiate a complaint or an issue.
2. Respond to an attack or criticism with a reflective listening statement.
3. Bring the conversation back to the basic issue.

Strategic Communication Techniques

It's pretty difficult for most of us to remain calm and in control when we're being attacked. Because we don't like an attack on our adequacy as a parent or a person, we generally shift into a defensive and angry mode to respond. That kind of reaction and the ensuing response just fuels the other person's anger or frenzy — which is why a free-for-all takes place. And it's why communication breaks down, angry words are used, both of you feel disrespected, and nothing productive happens. You stop talking and your thoughts about your co-parent are very dark, maybe even bordering on the homicidal! Here's a better way to use the basic communication strategies.

Rule 1. Always use an "I" message to initiate a discussion about a problem or an issue.

"I" messages are so basic and so common and, by the way, so effective. Just think about what you would rather hear if you were talking to your co-parent.

Option 1. "Don't you care about your son? You're late again to pick him up. He's been waiting an hour by the door because he knew you were taking him out on the boat. But you probably had something better to do!"

Option 2. "I was really worried when you didn't come at ten o'clock because I know how much Billy looks forward to his time with you. I'd really feel much better if you let us know so I can tell him when you're running late."

I expect you chose Option 2 (if you chose Option 1, you need to ask your therapist why you enjoy angry conflict). The "I" message in Option 2 is a polite and respectful way of talking about how your child is affected by your co-parent's behavior. When you talk about yourself ("I was really worried..."), you're not attacking your co-parent, you're being respectful, and you're raising an issue — not attacking his or her character or adequacy as a parent. You're more likely to get a more respectful and less defensive reaction with a well-constructed "I" message.

Rule 2. Respond to an attack or criticism with a reflective listening statement.

Instead of becoming defensive or firing back with an angry retort, use a reflective listening statement to show that you're hearing what your co-parent is saying. For example, if your co-parent starts blasting you because you were late to the parenting exchange, it will help defuse the situation by restating what she is saying: "I know you're angry that I'm so late coming to pick up the children and you think I do this all the time." Your co-parent is likely to agree with you ("Yes,

I am angry that you're late to pick up the children") and may even throw in another zinger, such as, "You're right, and I think it's very inconsiderate of my time." That calls for another reflective listening response: "You feel like I have no respect for your time." When you use reflective listening responses, your co-parent's anger will be reduced and the two of you are likelier to start a discussion of ways to solve the problem.

Rule 3. Bring the conversation back to the main topic when it gets off track.

It may be tempting to veer off in other directions and talk about how she had an affair years ago, or how he abandoned the children in the past, or how she talks about you to the children. But most likely none of this is really relevant to the issue you started with. Therefore, get it back to the basic topic, but do this in a gentle and firm way.

For example, you can say, "I agree we do need to talk about how I was unfaithful during our marriage, but it would be better if we scheduled a time to do this. I think the problem you brought up to begin with is one we can settle today. What do you think?"

There's usually no benefit to letting the conversation go into dangerous waters filled with those sharks called hot buttons.

Real-Life Examples for Your Consideration

Here are some real-life examples from people in high-conflict divorces we've worked with. These examples will help you better understand how you can use these communication techniques.

"I" Messages

Andre: "I feel sad that we're not following the fifty-fifty parenting time that we worked out in court because I don't see the kids enough. What I'd like is more time with our children."

Susan: "I feel very angry that we never find the time to sit down and talk about the debts we have because having those debts hanging over my head is extremely stressful. What I'd like is for us to plan how we will reduce our debts."

Reflective Listening Statements

Harry: "What I hear you saying is that you feel bad because I bring our son home late on Tuesdays, and that means he doesn't have time to complete his homework for the next day, and you want me to bring him home on time."

Lisa: "You're saying that you're concerned about what Melissa is exposed to at my house because I'm having an affair with my neighbor, and you need her not to have any overnights at my house for a while."

Bringing the Conversation Back to the Main Topic

Shelley: "I understand that it's important for you to talk about some of my past behavior, but I wonder if we could concentrate on the problem of whether our son should be on medication."

Lynton: "I can see that you have more feelings about my getting remarried than I thought you might have, and I appreciate that we need to find a time to talk about that. Let's go back to the problem of us trading weekends now, please."

Quick Review

If you're stuck in a relationship with your co-parent in which you feel most attempts at discussion get off on the wrong foot and then go downhill from there, brush up on some basic communication techniques and put them into practice with your co-parent immediately.

Voice complaints or bring up issues with "I" messages.

Respond to angry, insulting, or disrespectful attacks with a calm, dispassionate reflective listening statement.

Don't let discussions wander too far off course before bringing them back to the main topic.

Communicating by Email or Text Messages

You haven't done so well talking to your co-parent in person. Your phone conversations have also been disasters. And talking in the mediator's or parent coordinator's office has been a total failure. So you and your co-parent decided that sending emails or text messages would ease the communication breakdowns.

But, alas, emails and text messages haven't turned out to be miracle cures.

You would think that relaying messages about your kids couldn't go *that* wrong in an email or text message exchange. After all, you are not face-to-face, you both have time to think about what you want to say, and really all you want is to ask a question or convey some important information related to your children.

How wrong you were!

So, why haven't these electronic discussions worked?

There are three reasons email can lead to more fractured communication (these apply to texting too and can actually be accentuated in text messages due to the character/space constraints):

1. Nobody told you the rules for email or text message communication. Even your parent coordinator or therapist thought that two civilized adults could surely exchange information through an email. We all use email to communicate every day, and it goes well. However, there was no attempt to inform you of the rules for successful email communication between co-parents.
2. Some of the same problems that occur in your oral communication take place in your email or text message correspondence. What we mean is that your emotions, your anger, your

resentment, and your bitterness can show through whatever words you're typing on your keyboard. And more than just showing through, you may deliberately type in a sarcastic jibe, a hostile remark, or some other reminder of your lingering bitterness. Once you've sent off a sarcastic or hostile comment, there's no taking it back. You can be sure your co-parent is going to pick up on any hostile remarks and fire back his own angry retort.

3. Despite your best intentions of using appropriate communication techniques, such as "I" messages and reflective listening statements, you allow your emotions to color your efforts at communication.

We've asked numerous co-parents to share their email messages with us. What we've found is that even when bright, perceptive, and well-meaning co-parents insisted they did everything right and used proper communication techniques, their emails were often way off the mark and left us no doubt about why their email communication met with failure.

Fundamental Rules of Email Communication with Your Co-Parent

- Strictly observe the format for "I" messages and reflective listening statements.
- Get an objective person (we refer to them as editors) to monitor and, if necessary, edit your emails before you send them.
- Leave out anything you wouldn't want your children, your mother, or your religious or spiritual leader to read.

Strategic Email Communication Techniques

Emails can be highly effective and efficient ways of communicating between co-parents. However, you must observe the rules listed above. In this section, we'll explain the steps to the successful use of email for discussing topics and exchanging information with your co-parent. We won't speak separately about text messages, but the techniques we discuss here for emails apply equally to text messages.

Step 1. If you and your co-parent agree to communicate by email, encourage your co-parent to agree to these rules and procedures. If only you follow these email rules, it will help but perhaps not enough good will come out of the emails as would potentially occur if you both follow the rules.

Step 2. Decide on a set of email ground rules. For instance, here are some ground rules to which a co-parenting couple agreed:

- Don't expect an immediate response; give each other twenty-four hours to respond.
- Employ the basic communication skills of "I" messages and reflective listening statements.
- Use email only for nonemergency communications; true emergencies should be handled by phone or in person.
- Don't write anything in an email you would be uncomfortable sharing with the whole world.

You may have other ground rules for you and your co-parent to consider, but these should be important ground rules that are put in place before you begin.

Step 3. After writing an email, ask a trusted, objective person (such as a close friend who can take a neutral position, a therapist, a counselor, or a religious advisor) to read it over, edit it, and return it to you before you send it.

How to Be a Co-Parent Email Editor

1. Make sure an "I" message is really an "I" message and not an excuse to slyly attack the other parent.
2. Be objective. If you think the email you're reviewing would lead to anger, defensiveness, retaliation, withdrawal, or more bitterness, then use a heavy red pencil (figuratively speaking) to edit out words, phrases, or paragraphs that are likely to be inflammatory or cause further miscommunication.

3. Make sure the co-parent is writing what he or she truly means to say and is sticking to the topic.

Real-Life Examples for Your Consideration

Here are some examples of emails that make some major communication errors. The examples of bad emails are followed by edited and improved examples of emails for effective communication between co-parents.

Real-Life Example — An Original Email from Roger

Sheila,

    With all due respect, this issue about Boy Scouts and piano lessons confuses physical custody with joint legal custody. The divorce judgment grants us joint legal custody and grants you sole physical custody. What this means in nontechnical language is that the kids live with you, but I share equally in their upbringing. Joint legal custody means both parents have a say in decisions affecting the child. My responsibility to my kids in having joint legal custody is that I actively participate in their lives and we share decisions, such as whether they will be in Boy Scouts or take piano lessons.

    I hope this clears up the misunderstanding about physical custody versus joint legal custody. And I send this with the best intentions to help improve communication between us in the best interests of our children.

Roger

Roger's Edited Version

Sheila,

    I'm very happy that you want our children to take piano lessons. I believe children benefit greatly from any musical training, particularly piano lessons.

    As you know, I'm really committed to Boy Scouts and I really think the kids will benefit from Scouting, just as they will from music lessons. I'm wondering if there is a way that we could accomplish both our goals: Scouting and piano lessons. If you have some ideas for how we can achieve both goals, please share them with me.

    If we can improve our communication about these kinds of issues, I think it will be in the best interests of our children. Do you agree?

Roger

Real-Life Example — An Original Email from Juan

Maura,

You have chosen to continue to cut off routine constructive communication regarding Jonathan for a long time now as well as block open phone access and communication between Jonathan and me. You don't understand our son at all.

I just finally got to talk to Jonathan for the first time in two weeks. Jonathan just informed me he is still not interested in playing on the football team. He would like to play football, but not on that team. You had no right committing Jonathan to Friday night football against his wishes and intruding on the little time I have with him on the weekends. You didn't ask me, you told me! Jonathan and I will decide if his playing football on Friday night will be part of our agenda.

If you force him to play on Friday nights, I will keep him longer on Sunday nights to make up for our lost time together. You must learn to be proactive with me regarding Jonathan and his schedule or you must be prepared to pay the consequences.

Juan

Juan's Edited Version

Maura,

I feel concerned about Jonathan playing football this fall. He expresses to me that he doesn't want to play on the football team for which he's signed up. I think it would be a good idea for you and me to talk about this so we can decide if Jonathan is telling us each a consistent story.

It could be that he's telling me one thing and you another thing. I appreciate you signing him up for football and I want to be supportive of him being involved in sports, but if we can talk to each other then we can both be clear about what he is saying to each of us and we can also be clear about what we both want for him.

When would be a good time for us to talk without Jonathan around?

Juan

Real-Life Example — An Original Email from Jeanette

James,

I was wondering if I could have Cynthia on the weekend of May 20. I know it's your weekend, and I'm hoping you don't have any plans already scheduled so I could just keep her that weekend. Maybe we could exchange another weekend. However, because you didn't pick her up at all during April, it seems being a good father who's involved in his daughter's life isn't a big deal to you.

Let me know about the May 20 weekend.

Sincerely,
Jeanette

Jeanette's Edited Version

James,

I was wondering if I could have Cynthia on the weekend of May 20. I know it's your weekend, and I'm hoping you don't have any plans already scheduled so I could just keep her that weekend. Maybe we could exchange another weekend.

I realize that your time with Cynthia is precious to you, so I know I'm asking a lot for you to change weekends. Please get back to me so we can try to work out an exchange that meets your needs.

Thanks for your consideration of this request.

Sincerely,
Jeanette

These examples of original and edited emails show how an email disaster can be avoided. Furthermore, you can see how an email that was very likely going to provoke an angry exchange has been transformed into one that is more likely to bring about a productive exchange of ideas and information. Although there is a time and a place to express your anger and indignation, it is generally not in an email when your intent is — or should be — to bring about effective communication for the sake of your child.

Quick Review

There are three reasons your attempts to communicate by email or text message may not work:

1. Nobody told you the rules for email or text message communication.
2. Some of the same problems that occur in your oral communication take place in your email or text message correspondence.
3. Despite your best intentions to use appropriate communication techniques, you allow your emotions to color your efforts at communication.

If you observe some fundamental rules for email and text message communication between co-parents you will achieve greater success:

- Strictly observe the format for "I" messages and reflective listening statements.
- Get an objective person (an editor) to monitor and, if necessary, edit your emails before you send them.
- Leave out anything you would not want your children, your mother, or your religious or spiritual leader to read.

Emails and text messages can be highly effective and efficient ways of communicating between co-parents if you observe the rules listed above.

CHAPTER 13

Practice Makes Perfect

W hen you're trying to communicate with your co-parent, what usually goes wrong?

You probably know very well what goes awry when communication breaks down, but here's an example that will undoubtedly remind you about some of your failed attempts at communication with your co-parent.

Benjamin was prepared to have a pleasant conversation with Brittany, from whom he'd been divorced for two years. Benjamin felt like they needed to talk about their holiday schedule for Thanksgiving Day and Christmas. Even though their court order spelled out the holiday schedule in general, it left enough loopholes that Benjamin and Brittany had problems each year with the schedule.

To try to make their meeting as comfortable as possible, Benjamin arranged a meeting at Starbucks one Saturday afternoon in October.

"Thanks for meeting me," Benjamin said when they both had their coffee and snacks and were settled at a table away from other patrons.

"I know we need to talk about the holidays," Brittany said, "because I don't think either one of us wants a fiasco like last year."

"You've got that right," Benjamin agreed. "I think we can work this out fairly easily."

"Okay," Brittany said smiling, "where shall we begin?"

"Well, how about if we start with Thanksgiving and you tell me what you want to do," Benjamin said.

"Okay," said Brittany. "As you know my parents and my brother always come into town for Thanksgiving and they want to spend time with the girls. So, I'd like to have the girls from late Thanksgiving Day morning until about eight o'clock at night."

"Whoa, wait a minute," Benjamin said. "Let's back up. Our court order says . . ."

"Forget the court order," Brittany said. "I thought that's why we were talking: to deal with this and sort of figure out what would work for us. We both agreed the court order isn't really all that helpful on this issue."

"Maybe," Benjamin said, "but we have to start somewhere."

"Yes, I know," said Brittany. "But you asked me what I wanted, and I'm telling you, and you're saying you don't want to hear what I have to say..."

"Now, hold on! I didn't say that..."

"Then what are you saying?" asked Brittany. The tears in the corner of her eyes indicated she was getting frustrated already. "Are you saying the girls can't see my family on Thanksgiving?"

"No, nothing like that," said Benjamin, the edge in his voice suggesting he was starting to feel frustrated too. "I just think this should be a fair arrangement."

"Fair! When did you ever worry about things being fair? You always make sure our girls get to be with your family on the holidays, but you never think about my family!"

"See, you always do this when we try to talk about things we need to work out," said Benjamin. "You always accuse me of things that aren't true."

They stared at each other, silent for a few moments.

"All right," said Brittany with a sigh. "Can we try not to get so emotional and try to figure out how we can do this?"

"Yes," said Benjamin, "let's start over. So, you want the girls from the morning to the evening on Thanksgiving. But when do I get to spend Thanksgiving with them?"

"You can have them on Thanksgiving Day Eve and after eight o'clock on Thanksgiving Day."

"No!" Benjamin said. "That just won't work. My family can only get together on Thanksgiving Day, and I'd like them to be around my family too."

"You don't even like your family," Brittany said. "What difference does it make?"

"It makes a big difference to me," Benjamin said. "Look, this isn't working. I don't think we can do this on our own."

"As long as you're going to try to control things, I don't think we can work out anything!" returned Brittany.

"It's not about me trying to control things," Benjamin said. "What about you not knowing how to be fair. You're so self-centered!"

"You know what?" Brittany said, getting up and grabbing her jacket. "I'm out of here!"

With that, she departed and Benjamin was left sitting at Starbucks wondering how things went so wrong.

Just as perhaps you have learned from your interactions with your co-parent, we've seen over and over that because of the emotions you and your co-parent bring to a discussion, you can't be trusted to stick to

the business at hand. You may start out with the best of intentions —
as Benjamin and Brittany did — but feelings and old hurts or mistrust
get in the way, and the conversation gets derailed.

Take this brief attempt at a conversation between Leroy and Janice.

"I'm calling to let you know that I have the next week off from work,"
Janice said in initiating a phone call with Leroy. "So you won't have to
take Carly to daycare on Monday and Wednesday. We can both save
some driving time and money."

"Does that mean I don't get to see Carly at all this week?" Leroy asked.

"No, of course, not," Janice replied. "You can still see her as usual."

"Yeah, right," Leroy said sarcastically. "The last time you did me a
favor I missed out on time with her."

"Why do you always have to start an argument?" Janice asked. "I was
just trying to give you a heads up."

"Look, why don't you just meet me at her daycare on Monday and
Wednesday and you can pick her up there," Leroy suggested.

"That's ridiculous!" shouted Janice. "Why should I have to drive to
the daycare when you can bring her here?"

"Because our agreement says that I drop her off at daycare on
Mondays and Wednesdays."

"You are such a jerk!" Janice said as she slammed down the phone.

Old Hurts and Other Feelings Get in the Way

Janice seemed to have the best intentions in calling Leroy. However, he
suspected an ulterior motive on Janice's part, so he sabotaged what Janice
thought was a good idea and a kind gesture. That's what happens between
a lot of couples when they are in a high-conflict relationship. You tend to
carry around resentments, hurts, bitterness, hostility, and, perhaps, a great
deal of mistrust — just like both Leroy and Brittany. As much as you may
wish to hide or disguise those feelings, they often come out, and what
may have begun as a civil conversation degenerates into an argument.

Change the Way Conversations
Are Carried Out with a Script

You know what a script is. Usually it refers to the dialogue in a play
or a movie. The actors study the script and follow the lines just as they

were written. In that way, the other actors — and of course the director too — will not be surprised. With a script, everyone knows who's going to say what and when. And everyone knows where the conversation will go and how it will end.

The problem with unscripted conversations between you and your co-parent is that you have no idea what he or she will say and where the discussion will lead. Our suggestion is that if you want to make sure you don't veer off in the wrong direction or say something that will push your co-parent's emotional hot buttons you need to script your conversation ahead of time.

How to Write a Script

"But," you're saying, "I'm not a playwright. How can I script a conversation?"

And you might also be thinking, "I can script what I say, but I can't script what she says."

Both are points well taken. You're not a playwright, but you can write out what you plan to say, and because you know your co-parent very well, you can probably predict what he will say. Furthermore, you know what his emotional hot buttons are, so you can avoid those. The idea is that you write out what you want to say, anticipate her response, and decide how you will deal with her anticipated responses. You also know where you want the conversation to go and the goal you have in mind. Write out the dialogue in order to reach that goal, study it, and then use it in the real-life conversation. If you have to use notes or the actual script during the real conversation, that's okay.

Real-Life Examples of Co-Parent Scripts

Example 1. Chet wants to talk about a problem with their son.

When Frank, Chet and Samantha's five-year-old son, was at Chet's house for the weekend, Frank took one of Chet's wife's needles from the sewing room. When Carmen, Chet's wife, discovered Frank walking around with a needle, she was both scared and angry. She told him to give her the needle and asked him what he was doing with it.

"I don't know," Frank answered.

"Don't you know you could have seriously hurt yourself with that sharp needle?" Carmen exclaimed. But Frank didn't seem to get it.

Carmen grabbed Frank by the wrist and poked him in the finger with the needle.

"It's sharp and it can hurt you," she said. "Just like that!"

Frank yelped in pain and Carmen took him to the bathroom to put peroxide and a Band-Aid on his finger. When Chet got home, both Frank and Carmen told him what happened. Although Chet didn't think that was the best way for his wife to handle the problem, he could see what she was trying to do. However, he knew Frank would tell his mother, and she would probably overreact. Chet knew he needed to tell Samantha about this before she heard about it from Frank.

But Chet knew that Samantha would see this as an example of child abuse, and she might even threaten to call child protective services to try to get Chet and Carmen in trouble. She might even use the incident to request that parenting time be withheld from Chet. He knew he had to handle the conversation carefully with Samantha. He decided he would script it out to try to anticipate what she might say. He also didn't want to improvise this discussion because, he concluded, there was too much room for error if he tried that.

Here is the script he created on his computer:

Chet: I needed to talk to you about something that happened with Frank at our house. I wanted you to hear this from me first before Frank told you about it.

Samantha: Is Frankie okay? Did he get hurt?

Chet: He's fine, but we handled a situation in a way that may be upsetting to you. And I thought you should hear it from me.

Samantha: Okay, just tell me. I'm getting upset just waiting to hear what you have to say.

Chet: Okay. Carmen was home with Frankie and she saw that he had one of her needles that he must have gotten from her sewing room.

Samantha: And?

Chet: And he was carrying it around, when she saw it and took it away from him. She tried to explain to him how dangerous needles are.

Samantha: Is that all?

Chet: No, one other thing. She tried to explain how dangerous needles are and he didn't seem to be paying attention, so she poked him in the finger with the needle to teach him how dangerous needles are.

Samantha: What! She stabbed him with a needle!

Chet: I know it sounds bad, but it was just a prick and she made sure she put peroxide and a Band-Aid on it.

Samantha: That's the most stupid attempt at discipline I ever heard!

Chet: I know. I talked to her about it. And I think she could've handled this a whole lot better. I was just as shocked as you are.

Samantha: You're damned right, I'm shocked. And angry!

Chet: I really don't blame you. We both try to protect Frankie from harm and use positive discipline methods.

Samantha: We do; at least I do. I'm just so upset.

Chet: I know. I don't blame you. I'm upset, too.

Samantha: I don't want anything like this happening again.

Chet: I'm in complete agreement with you there.

Samantha: Maybe Carmen and Frankie shouldn't be alone without you there.

Chet: Yes, I think that's a good idea.

Samantha: Is Frankie okay?

Chet: Yes, he's fine. I'll be bringing him home later. And if you want to we can talk some more about this.

Samantha: Okay. Thanks for letting me know ahead of time.

Chet: Thanks for listening and coming up with a good suggestion.

In this real-life example, this was a situation that had all the ingredients for a major argument featuring a lot of defensiveness, threats, or even impulsive actions. Chet scripted it because he wanted to make sure he said things in ways that would undercut Samantha's anger and fears. He made sure he used reflective listening techniques, which we discussed in chapter 11. Because Chet mirrored back her feelings and showed that he heard what she was trying to say, Samantha had little reason to be angry with Chet. And because he helped to head off her anger, they were able to talk about how they would handle the situation. That was useful for both of them.

Example 2. Holly voices a complaint to her co-parent.

Holly, who had a contentious relationship with her co-parent, Arnold, had a problem that she wanted to discuss with him. She was concerned because their daughter, Missy, age twelve, had been on Ritalin for three years. Holly was concerned about all she read about medications for attention deficit hyperactivity disorder and wanted to talk about discontinuing medication. However, it had been a big fight in the first place, as they had disagreed about Missy starting medication three years ago. Arnold was strongly in favor of Missy taking medication. Holly had relented. But now she was concerned about the long-term effects. Remembering what it was like three years ago, and considering the many fights they had had about other issues since, she thought about scripting the conversation she wanted to have with Arnold.

Holly: I wanted to talk to you about Missy. Would now be a good time to talk?

Arnold: As good a time as any, I guess.

Holly: I'm really worried about Missy continuing to take Ritalin. She's been taking it now for three years.

Arnold: And doing very well on it, I might add.

Holly: You're right, she's done very well. And I have to admit that you were right to insist on her taking medication. I was against it, but I can see now that she really needed it to be successful at school.

Arnold: So now you want to take her off it so she can fail at school?

Holly: I think we both want the same thing — for her to be a success at school. I'm very proud of her success the last couple of years; she's really come a long way. And I think both you and she deserve a lot of credit for this.

Arnold: So why change something that's working so well. This is just like you to invent a problem where none exists.

Holly: You're probably right. Maybe I'm just making a problem out of nothing.

Arnold: That's what I think.

Holly: You've probably studied this more than I have, but do you think it's safe for her to continue to take Ritalin? Is there research that says there aren't long-term side effects?

Arnold: How do I know?

Holly: I'm really positive that you are a careful person who always tries to find out the answers to questions. And if you tell me that you've looked into this and she won't be harmed by continuing to take the medication, I'll try to relax about it.

Arnold: Okay, I'll look into it a little more and let you know. Okay?

Holly: That would be a big help. I would feel a lot better if I knew you felt it was all right. Thanks.

When Holly scripted this, she took into consideration that questioning the use of medication would be a hot button for Arnold. But she was ready for his angry response. She scripted it so that she agreed with him. She started out with an "I" message, and all the way through her conversation she took it on herself to accept responsibility for her worry and concern. Then, acknowledging his vanity and need to be right, she told him she would feel better if he could offer her assurance. She trusted that he loved their child as much as she and that if he said it was all right it would be because he did look into it and found out enough to reassure her — which is what she wanted.

Quick Review

When you attempt to communicate with your co-parent, often your old feelings get in the way and you push each other's hot buttons. Then those feelings derail what may have started out as an effective conversation. By scripting important conversations with your co-parent, you will have practiced what you want to say, anticipated his or her hot button issues, and found ways of dealing with his or her emotional responses. When you go into a discussion, you can have your script with you to have something to fall back on so you are not relying on your emotions to handle any twists or turns in the conversation.

Using a Format to Resolve Your Conflicts

During the three years following her divorce from Fred, Lorraine had primary custody of their two sons. In those years both boys had problems in school, and in the most recent school year each had failed one subject. This necessitated summer school, and Lorraine enrolled them at the end of May.

When Fred came to Lorraine's condo to pick up the boys one Friday, Lorraine told him she had registered the boys for summer school classes. Fred's response was quick: "Why didn't you tell me before you signed them up for summer school?"

"I didn't think there would be any question about them going to summer school to pass those classes," Lorraine replied. "But what we need to discuss is the tuition. I've paid the 250 dollars for each boy, and I'd like you to reimburse me for half of the cost."

"Wait a minute!" Fred said. "That's a lot of money. You can't just expect me to come up with that kind of money."

"Well, I sent a check for $500 to the school," Lorraine said, "and it's only fair that you pay half. They're your sons, too."

"If you were more consistent about checking their homework and making sure they did their schoolwork," Fred retorted, "maybe they wouldn't have to go to summer school!"

"Now you're blaming me for them failing their classes!" Lorraine said. "That's just like you! You don't know what goes on at this house. You just see them every other weekend!"

"Yeah, well you're always gone or busy with your friends," Fred responded. "You need to be more concerned about your kids!"

"If you were around more," Lorraine said angrily, "you'd know what I do to help them and how I supervise their schoolwork."

"I'm not going to stay here and let you yell at me," Fred said. He turned toward the car where his sons were sitting quietly trying not to listen to their parents' argument.

As Fred revved up the car and backed out of the driveway, Lorraine got in one last dig: "Just run away when we have a problem!"

This was a typical argument for Lorraine and Fred. When they tried to address issues, their emotions got in the way and nothing got settled. They were always more angry when they finished than when they started. Rarely were conflicts settled in an agreeable or cooperative fashion. Often their conflicts dragged on for weeks or months before some sort of resolution occurred.

If your attempts at discussing and resolving issues are similar to Fred and Lorraine's, you are an excellent candidate for a structured conflict resolution approach.

Structured Conflict Resolution

A structured conflict resolution approach has four distinct features:

1. A set format
2. Steps to follow
3. Prescribed language to use
4. A predictable outcome

A Set Format

The problem with the way most co-parents go about solving conflicts is that it is a more or less random procedure. That is, one person brings up an issue and depending on the tone of that initial statement or depending on the language and attitude of the response, the discussion can go downhill from there or it can be productive. But you never know. Is this time going to be productive or a complete failure? In a random approach, so much hinges on the tone and attitude of some of the initial statements.

If one of you starts out with an accusatory statement or tone ("I can't believe you let our son ride in a car with that alcoholic brother of yours!"), you can be sure that the tone is set for a counterattack and more angry exchanges are likely to follow. You both may be able to recover from this and go on to a productive discussion, but the chances are slim that this will happen.

On the other hand, if one of you starts out with an "I" message ("I got very nervous when I heard that you let our son ride in a car with your brother because I know he used to have a drinking problem. I need some reassurance that that was a safe situation for him"), the probability of a good dialogue goes way up.

A set format approach means that you use the same basic approach every time one of you wishes to bring up a problem, a conflict, or a thorny issue. However, in a set format approach, there are other steps besides starting off with an "I" message. These other steps are given in the next section.

The Steps to Follow

The following steps are very important in a discussion that will help you resolve conflicts with your co-parent.

Step 1. Start Off with an "I" Message. The initial statement should not be accusatory, provocative, or blaming. It should not enflame passions that will undermine a potentially fruitful discussion. In the example given above ("I can't believe you let our son ride in a car with that alcoholic brother of yours!"), this statement is more likely to start a fight, lead to a defensive response ("My brother is not an alcoholic!"), or provoke a counterattack ("You have no room to talk! Maybe it's time you started going to AA!").

An "I" message — in which you state how you feel about an issue and you talk about what your concerns are in a relatively nonemotional manner — is more likely to result in a positive discussion.

Step 2. Use a Reflective Listening Response to the "I" Message. The other co-parent needs to respond to the "I" message with a reflective listening statement. If we continue the theme we've started about the son riding in the car with an uncle who had a drinking problem ("I got very nervous when I heard that you let our son ride in a car with your brother because I know he used to have a drinking problem. I need some reassurance that that was a safe situation for him."), the reflective listening statement would sound like this:

"What I hear you saying is that you felt very nervous when you heard that Marlon rode in a car with my brother because you're aware he used to have a drinking problem and you need to be reassured that Marlon was safe."

That gives you the opportunity to acknowledge that indeed that was the point you were trying to make: "Exactly. I was worried about Marlon."

However, no matter how the initial problem is raised, a reflective listening statement is the most appropriate response. For example, here's how Sheldon raised a concern with his co-parent: "Why didn't you tell me you took Angel to the emergency room on Saturday night? You never tell me when something happens to our children!"

Almost anything that Sheldon's co-parent says in response to this may be defensive or emotional — unless a reflective listening statement is used. Thus, instead of responding in an emotional or defensive way, she could say, "You're angry because I had to take Angel to the hospital last Saturday and I didn't tell you. You feel like I don't tell you about things going on with our children." Sheldon is likely to agree with this, and agreeing allows one of them to go on to the next step.

Step 3. Indicate a Willingness to Solve the Problem. Once you give an "I" message, and the other person says she's heard and understood it, you have to say something like this: "I guess we have a problem here. Let's see if we can solve it."

When you've said this, the only thing left for your co-parent to say is, "You're right. We need to talk about this and get it solved."

One of you has to help make the transition from stating the problem to agreeing to do something about it.

Step 4. Brainstorm Ideas. Both of you can start throwing out ideas at this point to see what each of you think could solve the problem.

For example, if you were Sheldon's co-parent, you might suggest that each of you begin to be more conscientious about informing the other about events (like a trip to an emergency room) in the children's lives.

Or if you were the co-parent concerned about your child's safety in the car, your first brainstormed idea might be, "It would be important to be reassured that your brother is sober and not drinking anymore." To which the other person might say, "I think it's important that we trust each other that we both love Marlon and that neither of us would ever put him in an unsafe situation."

It's important when coming up with ideas to solve the problem that no immediate discussion — or sniping ("I knew you'd come up with something like that! There's no way I'd agree to that!") — take place. The ideas should just keep coming, and if there are several of them, it would be a good idea for one of you to jot them down so they can be remembered. Only when you've both exhausted all potential ideas should they be discussed one at a time.

Step 5. Follow a Pair of Rules for Discussion of the Brainstormed Ideas. Through our experience with hundreds of couples, perhaps most of them much like you and your co-parent, we have found that as part of the structured conflict resolution format, there should be some simple rules regarding the discussion and negotiation of brainstormed ideas. These two simple rules work wonders: (1) discuss each rule one at a time and (2) the co-parent who did not propose the rule gets first crack at the idea; however, only after a positive statement can that co-parent criticize it or revise it.

Here's how the discussion of one idea might look given these rules:

> *Maritza:* "Your idea was to not allow our son to ride with anyone if we aren't in the car as well. That's a good idea because it would probably mean we'd both be more careful about who we ride in a car with. However, that might be impractical. I mean would that mean we never allow our son to go in a car with grandparents or a babysitter unless we were also in the car?"
>
> *Gabe:* "Now that you mention it, I guess it might not always work, but I think we need to be very selective about who our son goes in a car with."
>
> *Maritza:* "I think we both agree with the basic idea: we shouldn't let our son ride with just anybody."
>
> *Gabe:* "Agreed."

Step 6. Negotiate a Win-Win Solution. While discussing all your brainstorming ideas using the rules given above, you can make a list of every point you both agree on. There may be some ideas you both agree won't work. There may be others you can't agree on that need to be discarded ("I can't agree that I should call you up every time Marlon will be riding in a car with another adult and discussing this with you first").

When all of the ideas have been discussed and you have several that you agree on, summarize those you agree on as your win-win solution. You should both write it down so it is clear that you've reached a solution on the same set of ideas. For example, Maritza and Gabe could summarize their agreement like this: "We agree that we will trust each other to use good judgment about who our son goes in a car with, we will be very selective about allowing him to ride with someone other than ourselves, and we will keep each other informed about longer trips that are planned when there will be another driver."

When both of you have written down this agreement, both of you should sign it and sign each other's copy.

Use Prescribed Language

Included in the six steps above is language that you should use to better ensure success. For example, in step 1 we recommend that you use an "I" message, and in step 2 we suggest reflective listening statements to let your co-parent know that you heard what he said. Furthermore, in step 3 we direct you to use specific language to indicate your willingness to solve the problem that was raised. And in step 5 we recommend that you both use positive statements when beginning to discuss each other's brainstormed ideas. By using this prescribed language — which has been tested with hundreds of parents in conflict resolution sessions — you are less likely to revert to comments and statements that will sidetrack the process.

A Predictable Outcome

When you use the four features of a structured conflict resolution approach and follow the six rules in feature 2, you stand a very good chance of having a predictable and successful outcome. That is the benefit of this structured approach. Maintain the format that we have found has worked for so many co-parenting couples, and you will be rewarded with a positive outcome.

Quick Review

A structured conflict resolution approach can help you be more successful in resolving conflicts with your co-parent and has these four features:

1. A set format
2. Steps to follow
3. Prescribed language to use
4. A predictable outcome

By following this approach, you will be able to move from a statement of the problem to an agreement to work on the conflict to brainstormed ideas, and, finally, to a negotiated win-win solution.

CHAPTER 15

Making Change Happen: With or Without Your Co-Parent's Cooperation

We're all raised to think that people only learn by reward and punishment. When your ex-spouse does something that you consider misbehavior, your instinct may be to punish, criticize, say things to the children, and in extreme instances go back to court. Often, you hope that the court will punish your co-parent; however, as you have likely learned by now, it usually doesn't work out that way. Courts deal with right and wrong only as it is related to what the law says. The court doesn't tell individuals that they're being mean and, therefore, they need to be nice. Or that because of their meanness their parenting time is going to be reduced. Or even that because they're not acting in a mature manner their parenting time will now be supervised. Unless a law has been violated, the court is unlikely to take any action.

In various other chapters in this book, we've discussed the idea that the only true power you have to change your co-parent's attitudes and behaviors is by changing yourself. This isn't a fancy psychological attempt to blame you for your co-parent's behavior. Neither is it an attempt to send you to therapy to find out what's wrong with you. We're not assuming there's anything wrong with you. In all likelihood, you're guilty of one thing and one thing only: you're guilty of being human.

Humans are cursed with a brain that prefers it when things fall into patterns. We like things to go the way they always have, and we take comfort in this repetition. In an odd way, we take comfort in that repetition even when things turn out badly. We feel reassured when we have the right to say, "There he goes again," but we don't stop long enough to also notice that "There I went again."

Alice came for therapy for her three children. Alice was a thirty-four-year-old woman who had been divorced from Phillip for two years. She was aware that Phillip continued to be unhappy and bitter because she had left him. However, she believed that her fourteen-year-old daughter, Steffani, was affected because Phillip asked her many questions about what her mother was doing. In addition, her father confided in her about aspects of the marriage and divorce. He told Steffani that it was her mother's idea to get the divorce and that he believed she'd been having an affair during the marriage. He told Steffani that the man Alice was currently dating was the man who broke up their marriage, although Alice said this wasn't at all true. Phillip also told Steffani that her mother was stealing his money and spending it on her boyfriend.

Alice was less concerned about the two younger children, who seemed oblivious to the things their father said. Steffani, however, had become more and more hostile toward Alice over the past six months. Steffani would come home from each visit with questions and challenges for her mother that usually started with "Dad said . . ." Alice would patiently explain to Steffani what parts of those things her father told her were true and what parts were false. Alice felt cornered by Phillip's accusations and didn't want her daughter to believe lies that were meant to make her look bad.

Alice continued this approach to the problem she believed Phillip was creating, but she reported to her therapist that there had been no improvement in Steffani's moods. Alice continued to tell Steffani "the truth" with the hope that Steffani would eventually see the light and understand that her father was lying. In fact, Steffani's moods got worse, and she challenged and verbally attacked her mother more aggressively. Alice was doing what logic and reason told her was the right thing to do, but the objective evidence suggested that her method of honest communication was making Steffani's moods worse.

Analyzing the Unproductive Cycle of Communication

Here's how we would analyze what was happening in Alice and Phillip's family.

Tactic 1. Alice tries to talk to Phillip but he won't speak to her. His unwillingness to talk to her means that all messages are being passed through the children. Some of these messages are appropriate to come through the kids, but many are not. For instance, it is appropriate for Phillip to talk to the children directly if he wants them to bring certain games to play at his house. However, it isn't appropriate to have them tell their mother that he won't be picking the kids up for his regularly scheduled weekend, particularly if he plans to see the children on a weekend that Alice is scheduled to spend with the children.

Tactic 2. Phillip talks to the children, pointing out negative things about their mother.

Tactic 3. The most sensitive of her children, Steffani, can't just let it go when her father says negative things about her mother. Steffani is compelled to confront her mother. Each week she returns home confronting her more and more angrily.

Tactic 4. Alice responds to Steffani's confrontations by sitting her down and calmly explaining the facts of the matter so that Steffani will know the truth.

Tactic 5. Despite this rational, communication-based approach to the problem, Steffani continues to ask questions and becomes progressively more angry and moody. It should be noted that some parents in this situation respond angrily — just as if they are talking to their co-parent — and the results are very similar.

Tactic 6. Alice leaves angry messages for Phillip about what a poor father he is and how he's poisoning his children's minds. Although like other co-parents, Alice might choose to file a motion in court at this point, let's assume this is one of the times she doesn't and she continues the pattern.

Tactic 7. Phillip plays the voicemail from his phone to the children and shows them how badly their mother is "mistreating" him. This returns the cycle to tactic 2, where Phillip shares things with the children followed by Steffani coming home to confront her mother.

To summarize this cycle, the pattern goes like this:

1. Alice **tries to talk** to Phillip without success.
2. Phillip **says negative things** to the children.
3. Steffani **confronts** her mother.
4. Alice **shares the facts** with Steffani.
5. Steffani **gets angrier**.
6. Alice **leaves messages** for Phillip.
7. Phillip **plays messages** for the children. (This is actually tactic 2 in the cycle and begins it all over again.)

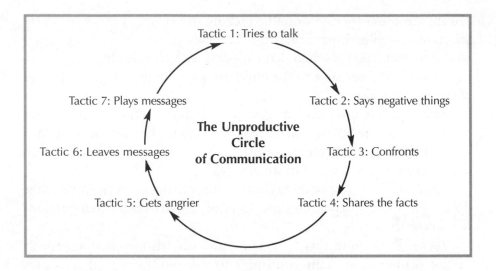

The cycle continues to repeat itself. Even if Alice were to file a motion in court, Phillip could use this as another piece of information to share with the children, showing them how their mother victimizes him — and the beat goes on.

Alice's Attempts to Punish Phillip Have Not Changed His Behavior

Despite Alice's punishment of Phillip (by castigating him on the phone), he continues the cycle. Also, despite Alice telling Steffani the truth and even showing her evidence supporting that truth, Steffani becomes angrier. Neither logic nor seeking justice helps Alice understand how to deal with this situation more successfully. If you find yourself in a cycle like this with your co-parent, you must ask yourself, "Do I want what's reasonable and fair, or do I want what will work?"

If your answer is that you want what will work, then we have some solutions you can try to change the cycle of miscommunication.

Alice, Phillip, and Steffani's family cycles through the seven tactics that we've outlined above. However, all of us, like Alice, are inclined to follow patterns even if they aren't working. Yet, each of these tactics holds a key to Alice taking control of the situation. If anyone in the situation does something different from what he or she usually does, everyone else will eventually have to do something different as well.

Doing Something Different

If you're angry, it will be hard to do nothing or to do something kind. If you still feel love for your co-parent, it will be difficult to respond in a firmer way than you usually would. If you feel guilty, you will have trouble not defending yourself to your child. Alice felt defensive and, therefore, had to explain herself to her daughter.

To do something different you have to make a plan to notice your impulse but do something that you've preplanned in place of your usual behavior. Let's go through the steps of Alice's attempts at communication and see how those tactics might be changed at each point using creativity and, sometimes, humor. Lesson 1 is to distinguish between those tactics that you can influence and those you either can't influence or can only affect minimally.

1. **Alice tries to talk to Phillip without success.**
   After several attempts at communicating with Phillip, it would be wise for Alice to conclude that additional attempts aren't going to work. Although Alice can't make Phillip respond when she tries to talk to him, she can alter what she does. Consider the following possibilities:
   - Stop trying to communicate for now.
   - Put the next message to Phillip in a greeting card that compliments him on being a good father.
   - Put the next business-like message, such as her proposed vacation plans, on the card that's stuck on a stick in a flower arrangement and have them delivered.
   - Communicate through a relative of his or Alice's who they both respect and ask that person for a return communication.

2. **Phillip talks to the kids.**
   This tactic in the cycle is outside of Alice's control. It is done between father and children when they are together. However, using a different option in tactic 1 for each attempt to communicate could throw a wrench in Phillip talking to the kids over a series of weeks. Change often takes at least two to four weeks.

3. **Steffani confronts Alice.**
   This tactic is also outside of Alice's control. It's based on her daughter's motivation to do it. Again, the changes made in tactic 1 may interfere with the cycle leading to this point, and Steffani may begin to change.

4. **Alice shares the facts with Steffani.**
   This tactic is very much within Alice's control. This is where she has some power and she should use it. Alice must first recognize that if she discusses the content of Steffani's accusations in any way, she is agreeing to a conversation about it. All strategies must focus on stopping the process of whether or not she and Steffani are going to have such a conversation at all. The goal of this tactic is to stop the unhealthy communication cycle. If Alice doesn't give useful responses to Steffani that keep the struggle going, Steffani has no information to take back to her father. In addition, once Steffani is removed from the struggle, she will lose interest and her father may discover that the game is over. In most cases, the parent on the other end of this cycle will stop the troubled communications through the children over the course of two to four weeks. Consider the following options for taking Steffani out of the struggle.

   - Alice could simply not defend herself.
   - Alice could tell Steffani that a lot of children don't know about these situations, and therefore she won't discuss it with her.
   - She could tell Steffani that this is adult business that she must stay out of and provide consequences for violation of this direction. This method may sound as if it will put Alice into a more negative light, but in fact it is different and she is acting like a parent rather than a jilted lover.
   - She could use the broken record technique. She can choose a phrase that she repeats as many times as necessary such as, "I know that concerns you, Honey,

but we're not discussing it." This technique can be used in conjunction with other potential approaches in this tactic.

- She could kiss her daughter on the forehead or cheek, say, "I love you," and walk away and do so each time Steffani approaches the subject again.
- Alice could give her daughter five dollars each time she comes home from co-parenting time challenging her. This method sounds as if it will reward the behavior but is, in fact, a confusion technique that can interfere with the behavior.

5. **Steffani gets angrier.**

If one or more of the earlier strategies is having helpful effects, there's a good chance this tactic simply won't happen. Alice is teaching Steffani that this communication and struggle is not her business by using the tactics above. As Steffani accepts that this is not her struggle, she begins to relax. When children and teens are exposed to adult business, it may result in what could be thought of as an emotional infection. They can't emotionally handle this level of internal conflict between two people they love and they become anxious, angry, or depressed or develop any number of other psychological conditions. Once removed from the struggle, the child's symptoms often improve over a period of time.

6. **Alice leaves messages for Phillip.**

Alice's options for this tactic are the following:

- Stop leaving messages. This places Phillip in a position in which he has no way to know whether his tactics with the children are having any effect on Alice.
- Leave a confusing message, such as telling him what a nice weekend the children had with him (regardless of whether they said this).

7. **Phillip plays messages for the children.** (This is actually tactic 2 in the overall cycle beginning again.)

There will either be no messages for Phillip to play for the children, or there will only be kind-sounding messages that Phillip will be unlikely to play. After all, such messages would not cast a negative light on Alice.

Alice could start at any of the tactics in the cycle and change will begin to occur. A family is like a pond. If you throw a stone into the pond, not only do you cause a plop in the water but also the ripples begin spreading out from the point at which the stone entered the water until the whole surface of the pond has been disturbed. This approach can work just as effectively with any range of behaviors (Watzlawick, Weakland, & Fisch, 1974).

Other Ways of Using This Approach

Consider the situation of Justin, who divorced his wife, Marika, against her wishes. She still loved Justin and used every interaction and contact between them that had to do with the children to try to build closeness with Justin and reactivate the marital relationship. Justin had no interest in reconciling with his wife, but he didn't want to offend her and start a battle, so he was unclear with her that he only wanted a business-like co-parenting relationship. Rather than take the children to the zoo on her parenting time, Marika told Justin that it would be good for the children to see them all together. She convinced Justin that a zoo trip and dinner would be best for them all. Despite the fact that he was uncomfortable, he didn't want to trigger an emotional explosion from Marika, so he went along on this outing and several others. After these outings, Marika stayed for hours at his house.

Justin needed to realize that by going along with Marika he was acting the same way he acted when they were married. Marika was recreating the marriage drama, and he was going along with it. He walked on eggshells around her temper and passively let her lead the way. Justin needed to find ways to begin to lead the way using his own personality and sensibilities. If he didn't begin to lead, he would remain emotionally married.

Consider What You Learned from the Approach Recommended for Alice and Phillip

Before reading on, take a moment to consider the case of Alice above and come up with your own ideas about how Justin could handle the situation differently. At what moments in the cycle does he have more power than he realizes he has? Once you identify these points, consider his options using the following guidelines:

- If it isn't working, he shouldn't keep doing it.
- Consider whether doing the opposite of what he usually does is possible. This is one of the easier ways to go.
- What could he do that would be out of character but not mean or provocative?
- What could Justin do that would confuse Marika so that she becomes unsure how to proceed to reactivate the romance?
- What could Justin do that would be humorous or playful and meet one or more of the suggestions above? For instance, what could he do that would be playful and out of character?

Take a moment to write down your thoughts about how you would advise Justin to proceed.

Okay, let's see how you did. We asked you to first identify the points in the cycle of interaction where Justin would have power to make a difference. Let's use the zoo trip as a typical example of how this couple has interacted in the past and see which moments in the cycle might offer opportunities for change.

1. **Marika usually drops the children off for their parenting time with Justin.**
   Justin could decide to pick the children up instead so that Marika's plan becomes confused.
2. **Justin assumes she will drop the children and leave.**
   Justin could prepare himself for Marika's usual response and rehearse within himself what he will do differently. For instance, he could plan to meet her at the curb and hustle the children into his car.

3. **Marika comes into the house and makes herself at home.**
   Justin could keep himself in the doorway and head directly for the car. He could pretend there is a deadline to make it to a show at the zoo and avoid conversation, leaving no pauses in his statements where Marika could respond.

4. **Marika starts discussing this becoming a zoo trip that includes her.**
   Justin could have other people lined up to be at the house and come along; these could be people with whom Marika doesn't get along. He could also act like he can't decide whether or not to go and say he needs to think about it. He could preorder tickets and not include one for her.

5. **Justin becomes befuddled and to avoid conflicts goes along with her plan.**
   As we discussed above, Justin could rehearse a wide range of options so that he isn't caught off guard and doesn't passively allow the usual dance to happen.

6. **Marika fulfills her desire to be with Justin.**
   Justin will have reduced the chances of Marika fulfilling her desire by taking one of any of the above actions. If he doesn't take any of those actions, he will have no control over whether Marika's desires are met, and he is, therefore, encouraging her to continue such behavior.

7. **Justin becomes more resentful but doesn't say anything to Marika.**
   Assuming he didn't take any of the above actions or similar ones, Justin can recognize that he participated in completing the usual cycle by not choosing to do anything different. He can then refocus his resentment from Marika to himself. He can begin to look at himself to see what is motivating him to continue performing this ritual with her. Justin may need to seek counseling if he's unable to figure out how to change some of his actions.

8. **Next parenting time Marika comes to drop the children.**
   This is the next cycle beginning again. Hopefully this cycle will change because of action Justin took in the previous cycle.

Think of These Ways of Intervening in the Unproductive Interaction You Have with Your Co-Parent

We'd like you to think about the type of intervention we're proposing as an experiment. Each time you live out the cycle, there are new opportunities to find creative solutions. In addition, you may have to keep repeating the same new behavior for up to a month before you can safely conclude whether or not the new behavior is being helpful. You may also get a reaction you didn't expect and that isn't ideal. If you get an odd reaction, first consider that this reaction may still be a good thing and let it develop for a few weeks. If the reaction isn't helpful, simply keep modifying your approach to the cycle, continuing to alter your choices with the knowledge you gain from the reactions you've gotten. A famous family therapist named John Weakland once said, "Life is one damned thing after another. Pathology (or emotional disturbance) is the same damned thing over and over again." When you divorced, you were expecting things to change. However, if your life is still "the same damned thing," you have the power to change your life to a life full of new and interesting damned things along with some great things as well.

Quick Review

Although you may want your co-parent to change because you see her as being the major reason the two of you are locked into an unproductive cycle of behavior, you can't directly change her.

But you can change. By analyzing the cycle of behavior between yourself and your co-parent, you can decide at which points you can do something different.

When you do something different, this will most often result in your co-parent also doing something different.

Special Considerations as You Continue to Try to Improve Your Communication with Your Co-Parent

CHAPTER 16

Improving Your Relationship with a Co-Parent with Special Needs and Problems

Y ou are probably thinking that this chapter was written for you, as you certainly have an ex with special needs. However, when we talk about special needs, we mean serious diagnosed issues that have or could have a significant impact on the parent-child relationship. Such issues include mental illness, substance abuse, and domestic violence.

For example, the following parents have serious special needs that affect their children.

Dave, the co-parent of two young children, has been diagnosed with bipolar disorder. When he is not taking his medication, he cycles between serious bouts of depression and extreme manic behavior in which he stays up all night, may leave the children home alone as he leaves impulsively to meet friends at a local nightclub, or may take the children on what turns out to be a wild, cross-country adventure without any advance planning or notice to his co-parent.

Francine, the noncustodial parent of a young daughter, has been battling alcoholism for most of her adult life. If she is in a drinking phase, she hides alcohol around her apartment, may get drunk when she is caring for her daughter, and has brought strangers home with her even though her daughter was sleeping over. Her co-parent is often frantic because he can't trust that their child will be safe in her care.

Kent, the father of three children, has been arrested on more than one occasion for physically assaulting his former wife. He stalks her, calls her at various hours during the night, and has threatened to kill her. Kent has court-ordered parenting time with their three children, but he is violent even in their presence. He once took the children with him when he was stalking their mother, and they had to listen to his diatribe against her as he called her vile names and described in graphic detail what he would do to her if he ever caught her with another man. Most of the time the children are terrified by his abusive language and his quick temper.

These three parents have special needs that have been diagnosed and confirmed by others. In this chapter we discuss various aspects related to co-parenting with someone with these kinds of issues. The most important reason for doing this is that although your co-parent may also have a special need, it is likely that you will still have to maintain a relationship with him or her. How you navigate this relationship, however, will help your children have a healthier relationship with you as well as with your former partner or spouse.

When you are co-parenting with someone who has a special need in one of the three areas we've mentioned — mental illness, substance abuse, or domestic violence — you may be subject to almost constant frustration and anxiety that will affect your children as well as you. You may frequently feel victimized and helpless in any of several types of situations if you don't find a way to deal with your co-parent that empowers rather than weakens you. Feeling like a victim will make you a less effective parent while it drains your energy and confidence in other areas of your life as well.

We've developed four steps that will help you be more effective in assessing and dealing with your co-parent with special needs:

Step 1. Determine if there is a real diagnosis.
Step 2. Evaluate the facts of the situation.
Step 3. Assess what control you have over the situation.
Step 4. Decide on a plan and keep it on a nonemotional basis.

Step 1: Is There a Real Diagnosis?

The first step in living with a co-parent with suspected special needs is to determine if there really is a problem, how serious it is, and how it will impact the children.

> Dominic is chronically late in coming to pick up his children. This drives Denise, his co-parent, crazy because she thinks it shows a disregard for the feelings of the children. Denise is annoyed and thinks Dominic is self-centered and uncaring toward her and the children. But however

much she is annoyed, being habitually late to pick up the children for parenting time is not a diagnosable problem and is unlikely to seriously harm the children in the long run.

It is common in divorce to throw around diagnoses of bipolar disorder, narcissistic personality disorder, and substance abuse. The thought that the children are spending time with someone with bipolar disorder can bring terrifying scenarios to mind; but are the scenarios real? How do you know when to worry and when not to worry?

Where Did the Diagnosis Come From?

It is not uncommon for lawyers, therapists, friends, and co-workers — people who perhaps have never even met your co-parent and often are not qualified to diagnose others — to label your co-parent based on their own experience or a segment of *Dr. Phil* they may have seen. People often go to therapy to help maneuver the stress of divorce, and as they share their view of their spouse the therapist may use a diagnosis to describe the spouse they've never seen. A diagnosis made without seeing someone is not a legitimate diagnosis. Now that psychiatric diagnoses are more in the mainstream, it is common for people to label those who frustrate or annoy them as having attention deficit disorder, narcissistic disorder, and, especially, bipolar disorder. Bipolar disorder is thrown around to describe anyone who is moody or has angry outbursts. Lawyers may latch onto diagnoses without checking out whether their origin is legitimate. Once a person is labeled, even if that label came from your neighbor, it is difficult to get rid of.

When Was the Diagnosis Made and Has Treatment Been Followed and Effective?

Just because your co-parent was diagnosed with depression and hospitalized as an adolescent doesn't mean that diagnosis still fits. Treatment, greater maturation, improved coping skills, and medication may have reduced its severity or even eliminated the condition or disorder. If an alcoholic has completed treatment and been substance free for a lengthy period of time, you have to trust that she will continue without constantly questioning the children about her behavior. We have worked with parents who trust one another enough for the parent with depression, anxiety, or even a substance abuse issue to be able to call his co-parent to say he has relapsed or is having a tough time and is getting back into treatment. It requires a great deal of trust to be able to depend on your co-parent to not use this information to go back to court in an effort to reduce your parenting time or change the custody arrangement.

> Justine had a history of severe depression that at times resulted in her staying in bed and being unable to go to work or take care of the house, herself, or the children. When she was not symptomatic, her co-parent, Bill, emphasized how good she was as a mother. When they got divorced, they maintained joint custody of their four- and six-year-old children with the understanding that Justine would let Bill know when she was getting depressed, and he would take the children until she was emotionally — and literally — back on her feet. Justine only had to do this one time but it was a big relief for both of them to know that Justine could be honest about her symptoms without fear that Bill would try to take the children away. They both agreed that by being open and honest with each other the children would be safe and soon have their mother back in their lives.

Step 2: Evaluate the Facts of the Situation

Was It a Problem during the Marriage?

This is a very difficult area to look at without emotion, especially if you are worried about your children. But it is very important to do.

How is the situation different now from when you were married? If you left the children home alone with your spouse when you were married, what is different now? If you allowed your co-parent to drive the children places before, what has changed since the divorce so that you now mistrust his driving ability? Is there any reason to believe the children are less safe now than when you were married? It could be that you have good reasons to be concerned now even though you weren't when you were married.

> Reed believed that his presence in the family relieved stress and provided the kind of stability that Dee needed in order to take her medication to control her bipolar symptoms. Once they were divorced and Reed was not there every day supporting Dee, she didn't always take her medication or keep her appointments with her psychiatrist. As a result,

Reed could not always trust that she was functioning well enough to care for their children.

———

During Raechelle's marriage with Charles, she tried to avoid leaving the children with him if she was sure he had been drinking. On occasion, however, she did leave their two kids with Charles when he had been drinking because she felt she had no choice. "I had to go to work or else I would have lost my job," Raechelle explained. "Somebody had to work to support the family, but that doesn't mean I wasn't worried and very uncomfortable all the time I was at work."

Sometimes the children would call Raechelle and complain about their father passing out on the couch or acting silly. However, Raechelle had to admit that their calling and complaining was not a safety issue. Charles never left the children home alone, and he never abused them. Furthermore, he never took them in the car when he had been drinking. After the divorce she was reluctant to leave the children with him for the weekend, but she couldn't justify keeping them from him then when she hadn't done that during the marriage.

If you felt that the children were safe with your co-parent when you were married, they are likely to be safe now unless there has been a change. Sometimes the stress of divorce does cause an increase in substance use or an exacerbation of symptoms that may require intervention. Most times these exacerbations will decrease as you both adjust to the divorce.

If It Is a Real Disorder, How Has It Impacted the Children?

Co-parents may have been properly diagnosed with a substance abuse or psychiatric disorder, but will this disorder have a demonstrable negative impact on the children?

For example, if your co-parent was diagnosed and treated for an eating disorder, such as bulimia, it might truly be unhealthy for her. It may be very upsetting to you that she binges and purges, but will this affect the health and safety of your children? If the children don't observe her vomiting after every meal, they may never know their mother has the disorder and she could be an excellent caretaker for the kids.

Likewise, if your co-parent is suicidal and there is the risk that he'll try to hurt himself while caring for the children, this represents a very different level of danger than the situation with a co-parent who was suicidal as a teenager and is no longer depressed. Children who live with a severely depressed parent may become anxious about the inability of their parent to care for himself. Or they may be frightened by his threats to harm himself. The parent's depressed condition could lead a child to become sad too. And if they are teenagers, they may resort to acting out or to taking over as caretakers for their distressed parent. Although limiting the time that the child is with the parent may be advisable, it will not necessarily decrease the child's anxiety unless the parent is doing something to improve his emotional state. If the court must be involved, the healthiest outcome for everyone would be that the diagnosed parent enter treatment in order to maintain or regain parenting time with the children.

Step 3: Assess What Control You Have over the Situation

Divorce Results in a Loss of Control

With divorce comes a loss of control over the other parent and the children. When you are married you at least have some sense that you have influence over the other parent. Out of loving concern, you can ask her to see a doctor or a therapist, go to AA, or take her medication. When you get divorced, things change — often dramatically. Not only do you no longer have the same ability to influence or control your co-parent but also now anything you say may have the opposite effect of what you desire.

No longer do you really know what happens when the children are with the other parent. This loss of control can lead to anxiety and worry. Of course, your anxiety, worry, and concern generally do nothing that is positive or productive. Despite your questioning of the children or your co-parent, you still may not know what is happening at the other house. In addition, you run the great risk of being accused of trying to control your co-parent, trying to spy on him, or trying to put the kids in the middle of your "obsessive concern."

Besides all that, even if you know — or think you know — what is happening at the other house, you can't do anything about it. If you try to do something about it, it only adds to the hostility between you and your co-parent.

For instance, if the children tell you that "Mommy is drinking beer" and you have been concerned about her drinking before, you don't know how much she is drinking — unless, of course, you enlist the children into being junior spies counting the beers she consumes. Bad idea! The more you involve the children in the problem, the more anxious you may become, and your co-parent may still be drinking her beer. Furthermore, now you have increased the children's anxiety, and they may try to intervene with their mother even if she really doesn't have a drinking problem.

What Control Do You Have?

When all is said and done, you only have control over yourself and your relationship with your children. However, that is still a great deal of control, and it is an important amount of control.

As long as you are not overwhelmed with anxiety and frustration because you realize you do have limited control over your co-parent, and as long as you are not a slave to other emotions and feelings, you can be emotionally available to your children. That will mean that you can enjoy your relationship with them, you can have fun with them, and through a loving and affectionate relationship unfettered with concern over controlling all aspects of their lives, you can have a positive influence in their formative years. The more available you are to them, the more they will know that they can depend on you.

For children to be confident and secure, they must have at least one parent who is loving and consistently available. As long as you are securely connected in your relationship with your children, you can be assured that they will grow up to be mentally healthy and resilient, able to cope with whatever other stressors life may throw at them.

Step 4: Decide on a Plan and Carry It Out in a Nonemotional Manner

If you have decided that your co-parent has a serious special need that could have a significant impact on your children, you need a plan for coping with it and helping your children cope with it.

Should You Involve the Court?

If there is real danger to the children, you do have an obligation to get the court involved. For instance, if your co-parent is driving the children while under the influence of alcohol or drugs, the court should be notified. Similarly, if the children are too young to be home alone and their parent is so intoxicated or high on drugs that she cannot function as an effective caregiver, the court may need to intervene.

You have to use good judgment to decide if the children really are in danger or if you simply don't like your co-parent's lifestyle. The co-parent with narcissistic personality disorder may drag his children off to his own sporting events at six o'clock in the morning every weekend or spend most of his parenting time driving to places he wants to go; but this is not endangering the child. On the other hand, if your co-parent is running a 5K race and leaves a toddler unattended, that is a danger. Also, the co-parent who takes a six-month-old baby on a four-wheeler is using poor judgment and may be placing the baby at considerable risk. But driving a two-year-old around the yard on the four-wheeler at five miles an hour may be against your better judgment but may not be labeled dangerous.

It takes careful and balanced thought, without fuel from well-meaning family, friends, and attorneys, to assess danger and to develop a plan for how you will try to handle the danger presented by a special needs co-parent.

How Do You Co-Parent with Someone with Special Needs?

Even if your co-parent is diagnosed with a substance abuse or serious psychiatric disorder, there is no one way to handle the situation, as there are mild and extreme cases of all disorders. Symptoms of bipolar disorder can range from very mild (moody and irritable) to severe (psychotic symptoms or extreme agitation). Medication may or may not adequately control the symptoms from a serious mental illness.

If the symptoms your co-parent exhibits are mild, you perhaps need do nothing. Although he or she may engage in very unpleasant behaviors, those behaviors may not endanger the children and thus may not require immediate response. However, how you react to your co-parent's special problems will be a model for your children in helping them deal not only with your co-parent but also with other people who may present special difficulties and challenges. The less distressed you are, the more stable an environment you create for your children. And the more stable their environment, the more secure they will become.

Try Changing the Pattern You've Had with Your Co-Parent

Try changing the recurring cycle you have been engaged in for years. It probably hasn't been productive, so you need to develop a new pattern of behaviors with your co-parent. Here are some suggestions for changing that pattern and for more effectively dealing with your special needs co-parent:

1. Stop attacking your co-parent based on what your children report to you. You can raise concerns with your co-parent by using an "I" message, but an accusation will only result in a defensive reaction.
2. Whenever possible, thank your co-parent for helping you out with the kids. No one wants to hear accusations or criticism. However, the occasional thank you can help warm the atmosphere between you.
3. Ask your co-parent's advice about something small. This is especially important if you have never done this before. It will help shift the power dynamics of your relationship to a more positive direction. Even people with mental illness or substance abuse problems can have good ideas about parenting and may know useful things about the kids.
4. Do not try to negotiate or argue with your co-parent if he is agitated. Wait for an appropriate time to express your concerns or raise issues. Doing this when he is agitated is the wrong time.
5. If you are unable to negotiate, at least follow the court order so there is less confusion and less need to negotiate at a time when compromise may not be possible.

Learn to Work around His or Her Problems

People are usually aware when they are in the depressed phase of bipolar disorder but not when they are agitated. Does your co-parent acknowledge any problems related to her disorder? If she does, you might be able to come up with a plan to switch parenting time when she is severely symptomatic. If she's willing to go with you, you might be able to use family therapy sessions to negotiate these difficult situations or even receive more assurances that your children are not in danger.

Reminders Can Be an Important Part of a Plan

> Peter was admittedly disorganized, and he was the first one to say he rarely checked his calendar for appointments. When Audrey, his co-parent, left a family therapy session early, he didn't know why she left. Later, he found that she was going to the open house at their daughter's school.
>
> "It would have been nice if she had reminded me of the open house," Peter said. "I'm sure I have it on my calendar, but she could have said something and I would have gone, too."

Perhaps your co-parent, much like Peter, was diagnosed with attention deficit hyperactivity disorder, and during the marriage you were the one who kept track of doctor appointments, sporting events, parent-teacher conferences, and open houses at school. When you are divorced and become responsible for only your life, your co-parent may miss events he would like to attend. What do you do?

You can nag and complain after the fact, you can let your co-parent learn (hopefully) from her mistakes, or you can continue to be the one in charge and send reminders. The first scenario will leave both of you as well as the children more miserable. Either of the other choices might work if you do not feel resentful of the outcome and if the children are not losing out on things. A combination of letting go — if it is not going to impact the children (a missed dental appointment can be rescheduled with little difficulty) — and reminders for events and activities that are important might be a plausible solution.

Reminders can be subtle or very direct. For example, Anthony, who was the parent who made most of the appointments and kept careful track of the schedule related to the children, usually opted for the subtle approach. For instance, when he wanted to remind his co-parent about an important soccer game, he would send her a text message like this: "Who is going to bring the snack to the soccer tournament tomorrow?" At other times he sent her an email listing the events scheduled for the week.

Quick Review

If you are in a postdivorce relationship with a person with special problems, these problems can lead to additional conflict. Rather than try to use these special needs and challenges against your co-parent, use four steps to determine the extent of the problem and the plan of action you should put into effect.

Step 1. Determine if there's a real diagnosis.

Step 2. Evaluate the facts of the situation.

Step 3. Assess what control you have over the situation.

Step 4. Decide on a plan and keep it on a nonemotional basis.

By following these four steps, you are more likely to determine whether your co-parent's special needs will have a significant impact on your children. If you determine that they will, you must have an appropriate plan of action.

Wrapping It Up:
You Can Be Successful
Co-Parents Despite
Your Conflicts

CHAPTER 17

Co-Parenting Successfully Despite Your Conflicts and Differences

When you're head-over-heels in love, differences between you and your heartthrob mean very little. You both may acknowledge the differences that exist between you, but you're so deeply in love you're convinced that you can either overlook those differences or work them out.

But give your relationship a few years and a gut-wrenching breakup or divorce, and those seemingly insignificant differences are suddenly magnified. What looked like minor bumps in an otherwise perfect relationship now are tremendous potholes making smoothness in the road to successful co-parenting next to impossible.

> When Maya and Jerome fell in love, it didn't matter that they were an interracial couple. Nor did it matter that they came from widely different backgrounds or that their parents had sharply contrasting parenting styles. They were in love and that was all that mattered.
>
> Maya's parents were loving, supportive, and easygoing, whereas Jerome's parents were strict, punitive, and at times abusive. His father was untrusting, suspicious, and controlling, and Jerome's homelife featured strict controls, many rules, and unreasonable restrictions. His parents watched his every move and made sure he only did what they wanted him to do.
>
> After Jerome and Maya had a child, they became more aware of how their differing backgrounds would have an impact on their co-parenting and their discipline. When their son was three years old, battles began between Maya and Jerome over their different approaches to discipline. Maya saw Jerome as harsh and unyielding. She didn't think he understood their child, and she thought he was unaware of normal child development. Jerome viewed Maya as lax and unable to appreciate the idea that if they did not teach their son self-control at age three, he would be out of control as a teenager.
>
> Following their divorce when their son was seven, the differences between them became such roadblocks to effective co-parenting that

they were constantly fighting. They tried to enlist friends and relatives on their respective sides to line up support against each other's parenting methods. They filed motions in court accusing each other of being unfit parents. And each thought they had the right answer to raising their son.

It Doesn't Have to Be This Way

Jan and Bruce didn't end up with the conflict over parenting that Jerome and Maya had.

Jan fell in love with Bruce when he was a Marine Corps officer. She was impressed by the uniform, but also she thought he was handsome, smart, and dependable. He loved her pretty brunette hair, her sparkling wit, her gracious warmth, and her smile.

Once they were married, Jan learned that being an officer's wife was not easy. They moved frequently to different parts of the country, and she often didn't see Bruce for weeks or months on end. When she was seven months pregnant, they moved from Virginia to California. Then, just before she gave birth to their daughter, he was deployed overseas. She was alone in a new home when their daughter, Rose, was born.

It wasn't until a year later that Bruce came home to live for a few months. And that's when Jan began to understand what he would be like as a husband and father. It was impressive to tell other people her husband was an officer in the Marines, but it was not so wonderful for Jan to live with an officer. Jan was a spontaneous, effervescent person, whereas Bruce was a by-the-book soldier who wanted to live — and raise their daughter — by a strict schedule. That led to arguments — and eventually a divorce.

Their differences didn't subside when they got a divorce. However, Jan was determined that they would make co-parenting work. "I woke up one day about a year after we got divorced and said to myself, 'You can't change him,'" she said several years later. "I realized that I spent all of the years of our marriage trying to change him and never succeeded. So what I decided on that day was that if I couldn't change him, I could change my reactions to him. That made all the difference."

Both Jan and Bruce accepted that they had different approaches to life and to parenting. They drove each other crazy, but they also kept their conflicts more private and tried not to fight or argue in front of Rose. Although they continued to disagree with each other, it didn't seem to affect their child. Rose reached her late adolescent years as an honor student, an athlete, and a loving daughter to both her parents.

Differences in Co-Parents in High-Conflict Divorces

The obvious reason people get divorced is they have irreconcilable differences. And these differences don't magically disappear after divorce. In fact, as we saw with both Jan and Bruce and Maya and Jerome, those differences continue unabated.

The differences between separated and divorced co-parents may run the gamut of the normal differences between parents — those based on backgrounds, cultures, personality, temperament, and their own parents' parenting styles — to those that are more often related to the high-conflict divorce. These latter differences will include lifestyle, approaches to parenting, and the feelings they have toward one another. It is typical for co-parents engaged in a high-conflict divorce to have difficulty agreeing on almost anything. As Martin, a man in a high-conflict divorce, put it, "If I say the sky is blue and I have an affidavit to that effect from a meteorologist to prove it, she will argue that it is not blue and she'll find her own meteorologist who will support her position."

All of the feelings that go along with a high-conflict divorce — anger, bitterness, hostility, and resentment — conspire to bring about an inability to see eye-to-eye on almost anything, including your jobs as co-parents. You may agree that you love your children, but you will differ in how you would like to see them raised.

How Can You Co-Parent Effectively Despite These Differences?

We are convinced that no matter how monumental the personal differences between you and your co-parent, you can still be effective co-parents. We have three ways for you to bring this about:

1. By remembering your children
2. By using as many of the tools from this book as possible
3. By doing something different

Remember Your Children

When we're working with a high-conflict couple and they are entrenched in hostile and intense polar opposite positions with every intention to not compromise, we often introduce a simple concept with words like this: "You know what I know about both of you? You both love your children. And I'm convinced you both want the absolute best for your beautiful children." Then, we let that statement hang there. Often that seems to melt the frigid atmosphere rapidly.

You, just like most parents who are battling each other, feel much love for and pride in your children. And it is surely true that you have no malicious intentions for your children. But when you're caught up in the differences between you and your co-parent, and when you're trying to defeat your co-parent in whatever conflict is currently being debated, you may forget about your children.

But you can remind yourself about why you must get along with your co-parent. Recall that in chapter 9 we discussed picturing your children. That's what you may have to do — and do frequently. That is, you must remember what the relationship is all about. You wouldn't have a relationship with this other person following divorce if it wasn't for your children. So, reach into your purse or wallet and bring out a photo of your children. Remind yourself how beautiful they are and how much you love them and how much you want the best for them.

> Kirsten pictured her child recently when her co-parent took their son to the emergency room for flu-like symptoms without telling her ahead of time; in fact, he didn't tell her until they were leaving the hospital and he called her on his cell phone.
>
> "I wanted to explode at him and tell him I had a right to be there to help Jonah through this," she said. "But I thought about Jonah and how sweet and innocent he is and how he didn't need fighting parents on top of just having received an injection from a doctor. So I kept my mouth shut and thanked my co-parent for calling me to tell me what was going on."

Keep photos of your children by the computer, by your phone, and on your desk at work. Any time and any place you're likely to be communicating with your co-parent, make sure there are photos handy. And remember — it's about nothing so precious as your children.

Use as Many Tools from This Book as Possible
This book was written to give you as many strategies as possible to change yourself and your co-parent. Sections II and III have thirteen

chapters, each with at least one solid technique or approach you can use to improve your relationship with your co-parent.

Take these approaches seriously and try them. Even if you can't change your co-parent, you will be able to change yourself — or your reactions to your co-parent — so that there is less anger and less hostility between you. Work with the differences, don't magnify them to such an extent that you end up doing what we see many individuals in high-conflict relationships do: make a solemn commitment to themselves that they'll "never agree to anything he/she wants!"

If you approach situations with your co-parent with this kind of attitude, nothing will change and the hostility and conflict will continue — with potentially serious and long-term deleterious consequences for your children.

Do Something Different

We covered this in chapter 16. It's an easy concept to understand, but not so easy to do.

Why not? Because in interactions with your co-parent you will get caught up in your emotions, you'll fall back into old communication patterns, and you'll forget about your children. But, as we said in chapter 15, when you do something different and something unexpected, you are likely to change the dynamics of your interaction with your co-parent.

When you disrupt the angry, hostile, and unproductive communication cycle with your co-parent, you begin to make changes. When you make a change by doing something different, you may actually cause your co-parent to also do something different. When this happens, the two of you are on your way to doing things in a completely different way. You may actually be on your way to being a more successful co-parent. And remember — that's what it's all about.

Quick Review

The obvious reason people get divorced is they have irreconcilable differences. And these differences don't magically disappear after divorce. In fact, as we have seen throughout this book, the differences can continue unabated for years.

However, we are convinced that no matter how monumental the personal differences between you and your co-parent, you can still be effective co-parents. There are three ways for you to bring this about:

1. By remembering that it's about your children
2. By using as many of the tools from this book as possible
3. By doing something different

Commit yourself to focusing on these three ways, and you will be an effective co-parent.

References

Ackerman, M. (1995). *Clinician's Guide to Child Custody Evaluations*. New York: Wiley.

Buchanan, C. M., & Heiges, K. L. (2001). When conflict continues after the divorce ends: Effects of post-divorce conflict on children. In J. Grych and F. Fincham (Eds.), *Interparental Conflict and Child Development*. New York: Cambridge University Press, 337–362.

DiGiuseppe, R., & Tafrate, R. (2001). A comprehensive treatment model for anger disorders. *Psychotherapy* 38(3): 262–271.

Grych, J. H., Harold, G. T., & Miles, C. J. (2003). A prospective investigation of appraisals as mediators of the link between interparental conflict and child adjustment. *Child Development*, 74, 1176–1193.

Hallowell, E. (2004). *Dare to Forgive: The Power of Moving On And Letting Go*. Deerfield Beach, FL: HCI, Inc.

Hollenbeck, J., Williams, C., & Klein, H. (1989). An empirical examination of the antecedents of commitment to difficult goals. *Journal of Applied Psychology* 74: 18–23.

Iribarren, C., Sidney, S., Bild, D. E., Liu, K., Marovitz, J. H., Roseman, J. M., et al. (2000). Association of hostility with coronary artery calcification in young adults: The CARDIA study. *Journal of the American Medical Association* 283: 2546–2551.

Johnston, J., & Campbell, L. (1988). *Impasses of Divorce: The Dynamics and Resolutions of Family Conflicts*. New York: Free Press.

King, V., & Heard, H. E. (1999). Nonresident father visitation, parental conflict, and mother's satisfaction: What's best for child well-being? *Journal of Marriage and Family* 61: 385–396.

Klein, H., Wesson, M., Hollenbeck, J., & Alge, B. (1999). Goal commitment and the goal-setting process: Conceptual clarification and empirical synthesis. *Journal of Applied Psychology* 84: 885–896.

Kubler-Ross, E. (1969). *On Death and Dying*. New York: Macmillan.

Locke, E. A., & Latham, G. P. (2002). Building a practically useful theory of goal setting and task motivation. *American Psychologist* 57(9): 705–717.

Luskin, F. (2003). *Forgive for Good: A Proven Prescription for Health and Happiness*. New York: Harpercollins.

Niaura, R., Todaro, J. F., Stroud, L., Spiro, A., Ward, K. D., & Weiss, S. (2002). Hostility, the metabolic syndrome, and incident coronary heart disease. *Health Psychology* 21: 588–593.

Postuma, A., & Harper, J. (1998). Comparisons of MMPI-2 responses of child custody and personal injury litigants. *Professional Psychology: Research and Practice* 29: 547–553.

Potter-Efron, R. (1994). *Angry All the Time: An Emergency Guide to Anger Control*. New York: MJF Books.

Price, J.A. (June/July, 1989). New divorce rituals. *Family Therapy Networker*. 22–23.

Richardson, A. (1967). Mental practice: A review and discussion: Part I. *Research Quarterly* 38: 95–107.

Siegel, J. C. (1996). Traditional MMPI-2 validity indicators and initial presentations in custody evaluations. *American Journal of Forensic Psychology* 14(3): 55–63.

Siegel, J. C., & Langford, J. S. (1998). MMPI-2 validity scales and suspected parental alienation syndrome. *American Journal of Forensic Psychology* 16(4): 5–14.

Steigerwald, F., and Stone, D. (1999). Cognitive restructuring and the 12-step program of Alcoholics Anonymous. *Journal of Substance Abuse Treatment* 16(4): 321–327.

Watzlawick, P., Weakland, J. & Fisch, R. (1974). *Change: Principles of Problem Formation and Problem Resolution*. New York: W. Norton and Co.

Worthington, E. L., Jr. (2001). *Five Steps to Forgiveness: The Art and Science of Forgiving*. New York: Crown Publishers.

Online Resources

Hobart and William Smith Colleges. "Relaxation Techniques."
   http://www.hws.edu/studentlife/counseling_relax.aspx
Lipman, F. (2010). "Interview with Archbishop Desmond Tutu."
   http://www.drfranklipman.com/archbishop-desmond-tutu
Rutgers Counseling and Psychological Services. "Muscle and Relaxation
   Technique." http://www.rci.rutgers.edu/~rccc/Relax.htm
The Guide to Psychology and Its Practice. "Progressive Muscle Relaxation."
   http://www.guidetopsychology.com/pmr.htm
The Quotations Page. "Mahatma Gandhi" (1994-2007).
   http://www.quotationspage.com/quote/2188.html
University of Maryland Sleep Disorders Clinic. "Five Relaxation Procedures."
   http://www.umm.edu/sleep/relax_tech.htm

Index

Parenting After Divorce: *Resolving Conflicts and Meeting Your Children's Needs* (Second Edition)
Philip M. Stahl, Ph.D.
Softcover: $17.95   208 pages   ISBN: 978-1-886230-84-2
Expert custody evaluator shows parents how to settle their differences in the best interests of their children. Offers practical help for divorcing parents, custody evaluators, family court counselors, marriage and family therapists, and others interested in the well-being of children.

After Your Divorce
Creating the Good Life on Your Own
Cynthia MacGregor and Robert E. Alberti, Ph.D.
Softcover: $16.95   272 pages   ISBN: 978-1-886230-77-4
Help for women in the process of establishing a new life after divorce: practical matters (finances, home maintenance), dealing with your ex (be assertive), helping your children to cope ("we didn't divorce you!"), and much, much more.

Rebuilding
When Your Relationship Ends (Third Edition)
Bruce Fisher, Ed.D. and Robert E. Alberti, Ph.D.
Softcover: $17.95   304 pages   ISBN: 978-1-886230-69-9
The most popular guide to divorce recovery. The "divorce process rebuilding blocks" format offers a nineteen-step process for putting life back together after divorce. Just the right balance of shoulder-to-cry-on and kick-in-the-pants self-help!

The Child Custody Book
How to Protect Your Children and Win Your Case
Judge James W. Stewart
Softcover: $17.95   192 pages   ISBN: 978-1-886230-27-9
Explains the process of court child custody litigation, showing how custody decisions are made, what can be expected at each stage of the process. Helps eliminate surprises that could lead to costly mistakes along the way.

Please see the following page for more books.

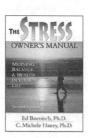